Quinn.

to chase the Best version of you!

COREY BAKER

Chasing
Better

AWAKENING THE PERSON YOU
HAVE ALWAYS LONGED TO BE

Printed in the United States of America

First Printing, 2018

Print ISBN: 978-1-54395-028-1
eBook ISBN: 978-1-54395-029-8

Book Baby Publishing

www.coreybaker.us

Design by Jeremy Wells

TABLE OF CONTENTS

Forward   1

Introduction   3

Chapter 1: Fear   6

Chapter 2: What others think   18

Chapter 3: Coaching   32

Chapter 4: Reading   41

Chapter 5: Money   54

Chapter 6: Health   68

Chapter 7: All the way there   81

Chapter 8: One thing we can all chase better   93

Chapter 9: Encouragement   105

Chapter 10: Communication   116

Chapter 11: The best parking attendant in the world   128

Chapter 12: Shut up and dance   138

Appendix   146

Acknowledgements   148

FORWARD

HONESTLY, I HAVE NEVER BEEN MUCH OF A READER, MAINLY BECAUSE I'M GREAT AT START-ing things but not finishing them, and that includes books. I would say part of that is on me. It takes a lot to grab and keep my attention.

However, I have never been more excited than I am right now. From the moment I picked up *Chasing Better*, I did not put the book down. I literally read it from start to finish, all in one sitting. Why? Well, we all know there is an elephant in every room, and Corey has a loving way of identifying the elephant around the topic covered in each chapter and then talking about it. The best part is that he shares with us his own personal experience of conquering fears, worrying about what others might think, and how we view money, just to name a few! Then, even better, he shares with us how he personally moved through each challenge. It's very rare that you find an author who will dive into the deep end of the pool and speak on topics that challenge concepts like the way we were brought up or the way we have always thought, concepts that may no longer be true or serving us.

In *Chasing Better*, Corey helped me realize that I am really just like most other husbands, fathers, leaders, pastors, and entrepreneurs in America. We are trying to figure out this thing called LIFE, while we daily chase the better version of ourselves, so that we can grow, become, and serve at a higher level as we walk out our purposes.

As you read *Chasing Better*, be prepared to have many of your own "I get you," or "I have felt the same way," or "No way! I thought I was the only one who dealt with that!" type of moments. The best part is that Corey gives specific, measurable actions, thoughts, ideas, and ways to start and continue chasing the better version of you so that you are equipped to expand your purpose and become better.

Doug Wood
Entrepreneur

INTRODUCTION

SO LET'S JUST GET THIS OUT OF THE WAY RIGHT OFF THE BAT. WHAT IN THE WORLD IS *Chasing Better* about? Who in the world is Corey Baker? Why should I care about either?

Great questions, and I truthfully appreciate your candor in even asking. Let's be honest: Amazon isn't lacking in the self-help book category. You could go to your local bookstore and have your fill of amazing options to help you. Are bookstores still a thing?

Allow me to take a few minutes to answer these questions. Here's what I know: If you are anything like me, you have STACKS of books that are on your to-read list and sitting on your desk, nightstand, or coffee table, most likely all of the above. The idea of adding another book to that list probably overwhelms you a little bit. You've got bookmarks in all of them somewhere around Chapter 3 and are just waiting for the inspiration to get them all finished. Isn't it so much fun to start reading a book? Finishing them is challenging, though, isn't it?

So why this book? Most likely, I don't know you. And, even if you are one of the people I do know personally and are reading this book, I don't know everything that makes you tick. I'm going to make a few observations about you without even knowing you. Can I do that? Of course I can. I'm writing this. I can say whatever I want! This could be trouble.

Here's what I think: I think you want to be better. I think you aren't satisfied with where you are in your life on multiple fronts. Sure, you are grateful, but this isn't a book about being grateful. Maybe that will be what my next book is about. This is a book about you chasing better. I've never met one person in my life who was satisfied with every aspect of their life. You can make an argument that the most successful people we know have the biggest desire to get better. Michael Jordan. Tiger Woods. Tom Brady. Kris Bryant. Serena Williams. Yes, I'm a sports fan. One thing I can promise you: This will not be the last time sports are mentioned in this book.

Every one of these people has a few things in common. They are all champions at their sports. They are all unsatisfied. They all strive to be better daily.

I think you have more in common with Tom Brady than you realize. Sure, he probably has more SuperBowl rings than you. He has a CRAZY strict diet and a wife who is a supermodel. But Tom Brady also has a drive inside of him to chase better every single day, and I think you have that drive inside of you as well. We all want to be better; we just aren't always sure better is possible.

Who in the world am I? That's a great question. I'm just a guy. I do enjoy knowing a little about the person writing the book that I'm reading. And, let's face it, you probably have no clue who I am. Let's start with the basics. I'm a husband, father, coach, and Cubs fan. Like, crazy Cubs fan. Name my daughter after the Cubs kind of Cubs fan. True story.

I was in full-time ministry for eighteen years. I'm still not exactly sure what "full-time" ministry is, but it basically means that for eighteen years, I received my paycheck from a Christian organization. I worked on staff at a GREAT church in Florida for about nine years, and then I was the lead pastor of another GREAT church in Florida for nine years. I met some amazing people. I learned a lot about myself. And I made a WHOLE LOT of mistakes.

While I am no longer in full-time ministry, I am still a firm believer in mission. I wake up every single day trying to live my life to serve others. I attend a church. I'm involved in a life group. And I've signed up to be a greeter. One thing I can promise—I'm going to be the BEST greeter that my church has ever had. I can promise you that. ☺

I'm going to guess that for some people reading this, learning that I was a pastor made you trust me a little more. Others of you, it made you trust me a little less. For some reading this book, faith is SUPER important to you. For others, it's not. Here is my hope, that regardless of what faith you may or may not have, this book can help you. If you know me, you won't be surprised by this statement. I can assure you this book won't be churchy. I'm not sure that is an actual word. But, if it isn't, I just made it one. I feel so empowered.

Why should you care about this? From the very beginning of my life, I've always known I wasn't the most talented. I was never the most talented baseball player. I was never the most talented bowler on my high school bowling team. Yes, I was a high school bowler. If that doesn't scream cool cat, I don't know what does.

When I was a pastor, I wasn't the best speaker. I wasn't the best leader. I CERTAINLY wasn't the best counselor. One thing I have always had going for me, though, is a desire to strive to be the best learner. I wanted to be, and still strive to be, the best me that I can be. I cannot think of too many things in life that I care more about than helping others become their best selves.

I hope that this book challenges you. I'm going to make a commitment to anyone who reads this. I'm going to shoot it straight with you. I'm going to write some things that you probably won't like. You may throw this book across the room a couple of times. I'm ok with that.

The process of bettering yourself isn't an easy one. We are going to be talking about some of the most important things ALL of us could chase better. If nothing else, I truly hope that this book inspires you to find ONE area of your life that you can improve and to chase after it with the same tenacity as you would have if you were running away from something that was chasing you.

CHAPTER 1

FEAR

"If you want to conquer fear, don't sit at home and think about it. Go out and get busy."

—Dale Carnegie

THUNDERSTORMS

THIS SEEMS LIKE AN ODD PLACE TO START A BOOK LIKE THIS. FEAR. WOULDN'T THIS SUBJECT be better at the middle or the end? Isn't a book supposed to be like a great story that has an introduction, a conflict, and a glorious finish that makes everyone watching (or reading) stand and applaud for minutes on end? I think you've already read that book.

If we are chasing better, why is it important for us to take a few minutes to talk about fear? It's important because fear is one of the top killers of desire for anyone to chase better.

We all have fears. I know I do. Some of them are rational. Some of them aren't. What does it even mean to "chase fear better?" How can I get better at fear? And is fear something I should eliminate completely from my life?

It's been said that we are born with only two known fears as babies: the fear of falling and the fear of loud noises. Growing up in a house where I was the oldest of four boys, I've always been accustomed to loud noises. I'm just loud. I talk loudly. I watch sports loudly. I sneeze loudly. I'm loud. By the way—on behalf of all of the loud sneezers in the world, we aren't dramatic. We aren't trying to put on a show. It's just how we sneeze. I don't understand quiet sneezers. Quite frankly, I don't trust them. If you are going to do something, go all out. Commit to it. Embody the sneeze. Moving on.

Even though I grew up in a house of all boys and am used to loud noises, I certainly get startled to this day when I hear an unexpected loud noise. I spent eighteen years living in Southwest Florida. You haven't experienced a thunderstorm until you live there. Florida has more lightning strikes than any other state. I've been in thunderstorms that felt as if a lightning bolt had literally landed in my back yard.

It almost takes your breath away. Fear grips you for a moment. Nature is so ridiculously powerful, and in the moment, you find yourself afraid. My kids definitely are not fans of loud noises. They get into the fetal position, put their head between their legs, and cover their ears.

Have you ever thought about this? We are almost never the cause of an unexpected loud noise. That's what makes it unexpected. Loud noises are much easier to deal with if you expect the loud noises. Think of a concert, where DBs blare from speakers with frequencies so loud that the person next to you can be shouting something to you and you can't understand what they are saying. We aren't afraid of those moments. We pay hundreds of dollars for them.

This means that we are most afraid of things that we don't understand or cannot control. There are close to seven billion people on Planet Earth right now, and all of us have one thing in common: we like to be in control. Sure, there are varying degrees of control. But all of us want it. And it scares us when we don't have it.

Thunderstorms make me feel incredibly small and powerless. I don't think I fear the loud noise nearly as much as what that loud noise represents. It represents not being in control.

CONTROL FREAK

CONTROL REALLY IS A FAÇADE IF YOU THINK ABOUT IT. WE ARE IN CONTROL OF FAR LESS than we realize. We have cars now that can drive themselves, yet that car that can drive itself can't stop a drunk driver from rear-ending me.

I don't believe this is license for all of us to just throw in the towel and not care anymore because we realize that so much is outside of our control. One of the worst things we do as people is stress ourselves out about things that we cannot control. Bottom line: If there is something chaotic that is happening in your life right now, I think it is important to ask yourself one question, "Can I control this?"

Can you control another person?
Can you control the weather that is causing your plane to be delayed for six hours?
Can you control the stock market?
Can you control the interest rate?
Can you control who the president is?

You cannot. Just because I can't control another person doesn't mean I should never trust. Just because the plane is delayed doesn't mean I have to invent new swear words as I stew in disgust. Just because the stock market is volatile doesn't mean I can't educate myself and invest wisely. Just because I don't think the candidate I support will win in my state doesn't mean I shouldn't vote.

In any situation, ask yourself, "What can I do about this?" There are some things I can't change. I can't change another person. I can't change the weather. I can change me, though. Know what I've realized?

When I look at ANYTHING through those lenses, it makes me far less afraid. It takes the focus off what I can't control and puts it on what I can. I want you to list your top five fears right now, and I GUARANTEE you that they have something to do with something that isn't in your control. So, are you scared of the thing you are scared of? Or are you scared of the fact that you don't have control?

What if I told you that you do have control? It's just not over what you think. What if you focused less on worrying and more on creating?

Have you ever noticed the rabbit trails we allow our minds to run down concerning the things that we are afraid of? This happens mostly at night. Thank God for melatonin, otherwise I'm not sure I would ever sleep. Yes, I take sleeping pills. Yes, I'm sure that isn't the best. At least melatonin is all natural. I'm way better at justifying than you are. Trust me.

WORRYWARTS

WE CAN WORRY OURSELVES TO DEATH ABOUT THINGS THAT WILL PROBABLY NEVER HAPPEN. Growing up, my mom used to call me a worrywart. True story. Until the writing of this book, I didn't know that worrywart was a word. Like one word. I always thought it was two words. I thought that somehow, if a person worried for too long, they could develop warts. Don't judge me. Maybe I should start using word of the day toilet paper.

Apparently, worrywart IS a word, and it means: a person who tends to dwell unduly on difficulty or troubles.

My favorite word in this definition is the word "unduly." Dwelling on things is just what we as people do. Is it good? Probably not. But it's what we do. However, dwelling unduly on difficulty or troubles is what takes us from the normal category to the worrywart one.

Unduly dwelling happens when we start talking ourselves into being afraid. We start allowing what could happen keep us from doing something that should happen. Two of the most powerful words in the English language are the words "what if."

What if is full of possibilities and potential. I love to dream and imagine what could happen. The problem is, most of the time when we use the words what if together, it isn't to dream of something amazing that is getting ready to happen. It's to picture the worst-case scenario.

We allow what if to talk us out of something instead of allowing what if to talk us into the action that would be required for us to create it.

I am fascinated by the notion that if humans are born with only two fears, that means the rest of our fears are learned. We learn to be afraid of snakes. And speaking in public. And getting rejected. And failing.

I truly believe that if fears can be learned, that means they can also be unlearned.

RUDE AWAKENING

AS I MENTIONED IN THE INTRO, I SPENT EIGHTEEN YEARS OF MY LIFE WORKING IN VOCA-tional church ministry. That's a fancy word that means I received a paycheck for working for a ministry. I honestly very much enjoyed it. I'm blessed to say that I walked away from that "profession," not because I was bitter or angry or had been treated badly. I had a GREAT experience and LOVED helping people. I just felt ready to move into a different way to help and inspire people. More on that later.

I was elected as the pastor of a church in Florida when I was twenty-nine years old. Truthfully, I had zero clue what I was doing. To this day, I have no clue why the congregation voted for me. I had no experience leading a church. I was young. I didn't have a college degree. I had a lot of church experience, and I was a pretty good communicator.

On my first Sunday as lead pastor, I was in the lobby of the church saying hello to people, and an older couple whom I hadn't met before walked up to me. They shook my hand and asked me if they could meet the pastor. I smiled and said, "You are looking at him. Nice to meet you." I will never forget what they said and did next. They looked at me and said, "No, we want to meet the real pastor. The lead pastor. You are the youth pastor, right?"

I smiled outwardly but thought of all the legal Christian swear words I could come up with internally. I good golly'd them to DEATH inside of my head. But I smiled back and said, "Sorry to disappoint you, but, again, I'm the lead pastor."

They shook my hand, smiled, and walked out of the church and back to the car, never to be seen or heard from again.

Happy first Sunday to me. Happy first Sunday to me. Happy first Sunday, dear Corey. Happy first Sunday to me.

The next chapter is all about overcoming a fear of what others think. But this incident truly brought to surface this idea that I couldn't do this. I remember getting through the service, shutting the door to my tiny office, and wondering if I could do this. We stuck it out and pastored there for nine years, seeing our church grow from 150 people every week to over 650 people.

PERFECTLY GOOD AIRPLANE

WHEN I HAD BEEN AT THE CHURCH FOR ABOUT SEVEN YEARS, WE DECIDED TO CHANGE THE name of our church. We felt it was time to go in a bit of a different direction and wanted a name that really signified that. We decided on the name Venture. Venture means bold or daring undertaking.

I am not a bold or daring guy for the most part. We did a six-week series that we launched prior to announcing the change. Before each message, we showed clips of people doing daring stuff like jumping out of planes, bungee jumping, and surfing crazy huge waves.

Each week, I would comment how there was no way in the world I could ever do anything like that. The main reason is because I am PETRIFIED of heights. I love roller coasters now, but I was dragged on my first one as a teenager, literally kicking and screaming.

One of our staff members at the church, Sam, had an idea. He said, "What if we announce the name change with you jumping out of an airplane?"

I said to him, "You're fired," in the best Donald Trump *Apprentice* voice that I could muster. But the more I thought about it, the more I started to come around to the idea. What better way to invite people to venture into the unknown than by me modeling venturing into something that I was afraid of? And there was NOTHING I was more afraid of than jumping out of an airplane.

So that is exactly what we did. Sam and I, along with a video crew, drove about an hour away from where we lived, on a Thursday morning in September, to go skydiving. Sam was brave enough to jump with me, which I was grateful for. He didn't want to be that guy who suggested someone else do something that he wasn't willing to do. He's a good guy, minus the being a Packer fan part.

We got to the place. Signed our lives away on a waiver. Watched a training video where they told us it was possible we could die. And sat in the hanger before waiting for our turn to be called. I just remember watching the groups before us go. I remember counting the number of jumpers who got into the plane and counting to see if the same numbers of people landed in parachutes fifteen minutes later.

Finally, it was our turn to go, and it was a blur. We did a tandem jump, which means we had an instructor strapped to our back. That brought me some comfort. The plane takes off, and we climb to 12,000 feet. They open up the side door, and suddenly this idea is becoming very real. Our camera guy climbs out on the side of the plane so that he can film my reaction when we make the initial jump. The instructor gives me the sign, 3, 2, 1, and we jump out of an airplane at 12,000 feet.

We free fall for sixty seconds. You have no idea how long sixty seconds seems until you get your clock app on your phone out, hit start, and watch that number slowly tick to sixty seconds. But in the air, the free fall felt like it was over in ten seconds. I had a t-shirt on that said the name of our new church, and I showed our congregation via video as I was gliding through the air. It was EXHILARATING. I'll never forget two things: I'll never forget the feeling of relief when the parachute worked, and I'll never forget the feeling of relief when we landed and my feet touched the ground again. I may have kissed the grass. Don't judge me.

I learned so much about myself from this experience. I learned that I am capable of far more than I realize. I learned that I don't have to be paralyzed by fear. That's exactly what fear does to us. It paralyzes us. I want you to picture that you are on the edge of a cliff looking over the side as water crashes into rocks 1,000 feet below where you are standing. Have you broken into cold sweats yet? No? Just me? Okay then.

What happens when you get into a situation in which you are terrified? You freeze. Literally freeze. Dead in your tracks. Just like in the movies.

Fear does that to us. It completely paralyzes us and stops us in our tracks. Fear holds us captive from experiencing life-changing moments. Instead of saying, "What if I'll have a story to tell people the rest of my life?" we dwell on, "What if the parachute doesn't open?"

I'm not advocating being an idiot. Maybe that should be the sub theme for this book. The main point is to chase being better. The second one is don't be an idiot.

Now that I have the disclaimers and balancing statements out of the way, I can finish this chapter STRONG. You've already flipped to see how many pages are left before this chapter is finished. Don't pretend you haven't!

UNLEARNING FEAR

FROM THE VERY BEGINNING OF OUR LIVES, WE HAVE BEEN TAUGHT AND CONDITIONED TO BE cautious. Think about this: The vast majority of parenting a young child is more about teaching them what not to do than teaching them what they actually should do. We teach them to do things, for sure. We teach them to say "please" and "thank you." We teach how to say "more" in sign language before they can even speak. We teach little boys how to lift the toilet seat and aim at the cheerio in the toilet.

We teach them a LOT about what not to do, though. Don't touch the stove. Don't make a mess. Don't hit your brother. Don't be loud. Don't stay up too late. Don't watch that tablet anymore. Don't leave your naked Barbies all over the house.

I've said these things. Literally all of them, except the don't hit your brother part, because we don't have any boys. My parents told that to me, though!

The point is, teaching kids what not to do is part of raising them. But, from the very beginning, it seems as if we are teaching our kids to be cautious. The best part of being a kid is the feeling that the possibilities are endless and the world is full of adventure. Everything is a toy. Everything is a game. You are always the hero. And your sibling is always the villain.

Kids love color, but it seems like the older we get, the less we love color and adventure, and the more we love comfort and stability. We'd just rather play it safe. Kids are desperate to win, like, at everything. As we get older, I don't think we want to win as much anymore. We just really really don't want to lose.

What if I could play to win every day? What if I made risk a daily habit? Will I lose sometimes? Goodness yes. But the agony of losing is actually what makes us work harder to experience the thrill of winning.

What if, instead of running away from the things that we are afraid of, we ran toward them? What if the Goliath we are terrified of because he is big and powerful is actually clumsy and slow?

I want to ask you a super deep question. What are you afraid of? No, like, really, really afraid of. I know you are afraid of snakes. I'm sure heights is a big one. But, really. What are you afraid of? Rejection? Losing everything?

When you realize what that is, I want you to ask yourself how living with that fear has negatively impacted your life. What has it kept you from doing? What has it kept you from experiencing? Who has it kept you from trusting?

You know what the most freeing thing about this idea of chasing better is? It means that I want to get better at this area, not that it will never be an issue ever again. Do you know how to never, ever be afraid again? It's impossible, because the ability to be afraid is part of what it means to be human.

You aren't weak because you have fear. You are human because you have fear. This is not about eliminating all fear from your life. I think the concept of fearlessness is irrational. No person on planet earth is fearless. We just have some people who run toward their fears and some people who run away from them.

That may seem like a small thing, but it's not. Do you have things you are afraid of? Me, too. What if your fears didn't have to reveal weakness but instead revealed an opportunity for strength? An opportunity to get better at something?

So how can I get better at fear? What does that mean? The first step is just as simple as that—take a step and refuse to be paralyzed anymore. That's why I jumped out of the airplane. Can I let you in on a little secret? I'm still scared of heights. Jumping out of one airplane didn't eliminate that fear from my life. It's still there. I still get uncomfortable climbing up stairs to go down giant waterslides with my kids.

I'm still scared of heights; I'm just not paralyzed by them anymore. I want to challenge you to stop saying the words "what if" in reference to something you are afraid of, unless what if has to do with something positive.

Stop expecting yourself to be fearless. And stop thinking your fear is a weakness. It's only a weakness if you allow it to paralyze you. I can GUARANTEE you that soldiers who fight in battles are afraid every single time they engage in a fight. Boxers are afraid before they step into a ring with someone who could end their career or even their life with one punch. Athletes have fear before every game. They aren't just afraid they will get hurt. They are afraid they could make a mistake that costs their team a chance to win. Singers are scared they will miss a note. Stand-up comics are scared people will throw things at them. Seriously, who does that?

In spite of their fears, they step onto the field, into the ring, and onto the stage. Why? Because the possibility for victory is way more compelling than the possibility of defeat. People in the stands may not understand what it's like to lose the biggest game of their life with millions of people watching, but they also don't know what it's like to sleep next to a SuperBowl trophy.

That's how you chase better. You have to desire to win more than you desire not to lose. Winning has to drive you. I realize we aren't all in a game. We are all in a competition, though. I want to introduce you to someone.

Before I introduce that person to you, I want to ask you a question. Have you ever had to deal with a difficult person in your life? A difficult family member? A dramatic friend? A complaining co-worker? An overbearing boss? That's part of life. Every single one of us have difficult people in our lives.

You ready to meet the person I want to introduce you to? They will be by FAR the most difficult person you will ever have to lead in your entire life. That person is you. You, my friend, are THE MOST difficult person you will ever have to deal with in your life.

You want to know why that is good news? It's good news because you can't change those other difficult people in your life. You can change you, though. I've realized that I am the most difficult person I will ever manage in my whole life. It's made me have much more grace with others. Dealing with them is a piece of cake, no matter how dramatic they are. I have to deal with me every day, and that, my friends, is no easy task. You can ask my wife.

Just like with every other chapter in this book, when it comes to fear, we aren't chasing best; we are simply chasing better. I'm not sure who the best person is at eliminating fear. A sobering reality for all of us is that unless you are LeBron James playing basketball, there will most likely always be someone out there who is better than you at something. Someone will always have more money. More talent. You can beat them at one thing, though: A desire to be better. A desire to grow in every area of your life.

The next time you are confronted with something or someone you are afraid of, if you are afraid to have a necessary conversation with a person, breathe, pick up the phone, and call them. Let's be people who first of all identify the areas of our lives that we are afraid of. We all have them. You will never overcome or get better at something you can't identify. Step 1 is to identify it.

Once you identify it, your first reaction will be to be paralyzed by it and begin playing the what if game. What if I fall over the edge? What if the chute doesn't open? What if they never talk to me again?

Turn off those thoughts and begin taking a step in the direction of the thing that you are afraid of. You may not ever be a skydiving instructor. You may not be best friends with that person you need to have that difficult conversation with anymore. But you are no longer paralyzed. And you've taken the first step towards chasing a better you.

CHAPTER 2

WHAT OTHERS THINK

"No one can make you feel inferior without your consent."

—Eleanor Roosevelt

PEOPLE WATCHING

PEOPLE ARE SO FUNNY. DO YOU EVER PEOPLE WATCH? NOT LIKE IN A STALKER KIND OF WAY. Quit lying! You do it, too. We people watch at malls, airports, and sporting events. We DEFINITELY people watch whenever we have to go to Walmart at 11:00 p.m. on a Friday night. Judging others is just something all of us do naturally. Most of us know absolutely nothing about the person we are judging, yet we create scenarios in our heads that may as well be gospel.

Later in this chapter, we will get into how to deal with others being critical of you. If you want to be successful, it's going to happen. First, however, let's start with you. I read a quote that has been attributed to many people, so the truth is I have no idea who originally said it. I just know it wasn't me.

"We tend to judge others based on their actions and ourselves based on our intentions."

What in the world does that mean? I'm guessing there isn't one person reading this book who enjoys finding out that someone else has spoken negatively about them. Yet we think it's ok for us to do the same. People are hypocritical. I'm hypocritical. So are you. Don't believe me? I'll prove it to you.

ROAD RAGE

NOWHERE DOES THE HYPOCRISY OF MANKIND BECOME MORE APPARENT THAN WHEN WE ARE behind the wheel of a car. America suffers from an incurable disease of road rage. Some of the nicest people I have ever met in my LIFE are absolute maniacs behind the wheel of a car. This is exactly what we do when we drive. If you are in a hurry, and the person in front of you is traveling slower than you, you get IRRITATED. I'm talking the talk to yourself and yell at the driver in front of you at the top of your lungs to step on the gas even though they can't hear you kind of irritated.

We all have the judgy driver stare down pat. Don't look at me like that. You do it, too. You have a car that is in front of you that is going slow, and you pass them, but before you pass them, you give them a look. In your head, you are saying, "Yeah you better not look back at me. You know what you did, Mr. Prius. Do you have any idea how late I am going to be? Do you know that the speed limit is forty-five and you are only going forty-five? My grandmother drives ten miles over the speed limit, and she doesn't even drive anymore."

Let's flip the script. Every one of us have had someone behind us driving who is tailgating us. When someone is tailgating you, what do you do? You drive even slower; that's what you do. Why? Because in our head we are saying, "Dude, slow down." "Why are you in such a rush?" When that car inevitably passes us, we bring back the judgy "You are driving too fast" stare, as the BMW passes you in a flash with their tinted windows and WWJD bumper sticker on the back.

When we are in a hurry, everyone else is slow. And when we aren't in a hurry, everyone else simply needs to chill out because they will get where they are going eventually, and maybe they just should have left five minutes earlier.

People employ that same hypocrisy when it comes to talking about others. We can't stand when people do it to us. We think it's ok when we do it. Upset with me yet? Good. That's my goal.

I don't have an audience with the person who is talking about you right now. I do have the opportunity to help you by virtue of you reading this book. So let's talk about you. What I have learned is that most people who talk the most about others don't have a whole lot they are chasing as far as goals in their own life.

They don't think success is possible for them, so they have resolved to be critical of others. I guarantee there will be some people who are critical of this book. They will criticize grammar and word choice and content. Yet they have never written a book themselves. It's ok. I can take it. Criticize away. ☺

Don't be that person. What are you chasing? What goals keep you awake at night? What are you trying to create? Are you laser focused on growing your company? Growing your church? Raising amazing kids? Earning incredible wealth? If you are, you won't have time to stop and be critical of everything everyone else is doing.

You would spend far less time criticizing others if you spent more time chasing your goals. You would also worry less about what others thought about you because when you are laser focused on a goal, you don't have time to look to the right or the left.

BENEFIT OF THE DOUBT

BEFORE I HELP YOU GET OVER AND PAST WHAT OTHERS SAY ABOUT YOU, I WANT TO CHALlenge you to not become the very person you can't stand. The truth is, if you find yourself consistently talking negatively about others, your goals aren't big enough, and you are living too small. Is that what you want? You want to be a small person with small goals? If so, don't change a thing. I think you want to be better. If you didn't, you wouldn't be reading a book called *Chasing Better*.

If there was one thing I wish America in general would get better at, it would be giving others the benefit of the doubt. We don't do that very well. Our court system may be innocent until proven guilty, but the court of public opinion is always guilty until proven innocent.

Many people say the reason they don't give others the benefit of the doubt is because they have done so before and ended up getting hurt. I would personally rather live a life where I give others the benefit of the doubt too much and get hurt than be someone who never gives anyone the benefit of the doubt and never trusts anyone.

I understand this is a slippery slope. People ABSOLUTELY need to be held accountable for their actions, and there needs to be a system put in place where people can tell the truth. If you have been hurt or wronged, TELL SOMEONE.

I'm mainly talking about scenarios that we tend to create in our heads. You know what I'm talking about. It's one thing if we KNOW for sure someone has been talking badly about us or just flat doesn't like us at all. We will get into that option in a second.

INTERNAL STORYTELLERS

I'VE LEARNED FROM MY LIFE THAT I AM AN AMAZING STORYTELLER WHEN IT COMES TO inventing things that others could be saying about me. We worry about this way more today because of social media. We worry about who liked our post. Who didn't like our post. Why didn't they like it? Are they still upset because I didn't invite them to that concert? Ok, they shouldn't be mad about that. Seriously, I only had three tickets, and two of them had to go to family. Why can't they just be happy for me? I'm always supportive of them. On and on it goes.

Could it possibly be they didn't see your post in the first place? Even if they did see it, does them not pressing a "like button" mean they aren't supportive? Most of the time, the stories we imagine taking place never actually happen. We let our minds wander. I'm all for daydreaming. I daydream in the shower all the time! I imagine how I am going to invest all of the money I am going to earn. I imagine my Cubs season tickets and my indoor bowling alley.

Most of the time, our daydreams turn into day nightmares. I'm not one who remembers my dream often, but I can't stand having nightmares. You wake up sweating. You have a hard time going back to sleep. Not fun.

We willingly put ourselves through day nightmares when we sit and invent theories about what people think about us. The more we think about it, the more upset we get with the person whom we perceive to be saying such "atrocities."

The truth is, the vast majority of the time when we think someone is talking about us or thinking negatively about us, they really aren't. You know what they are thinking about? Themselves. People love thinking about themselves and really love talking about themselves. Ever been in a situation where you are having a conversation with someone and it feels awkward or stagnant? Maybe on a sales call with a perspective client or a first date with a potential significant other? Just start asking them questions about them, and they will start talking. It's human nature.

The most likely scenario is that people aren't talking about you. They aren't talking about you because they aren't thinking about you. Let's say they are. Let's say you have a full-blown hater.

HATERS GONNA HATE

APPARENTLY, HATER IS ACTUALLY A WORD. IT'S ACTUALLY IN THE DICTIONARY. PROBABLY THE revised version, because I can't imagine Thomas Jefferson calling John Adams a "hater."

I could just read you the dictionary definition of hater, but that would be boring. Instead, I will do something better. I am going to read you the definition of hater from the Urban Dictionary. If you have never explored the Urban Dictionary, you are missing out. I've never in my life been told that I come close to resembling anything Urban. I'm pasty. I'm white. I'm a tad on the dorky side. Let's just call a spade a spade. Here's how Urban Dictionary defines hater:

"A person that simply cannot be happy for another person's success. So rather than be happy they make a point of exposing a flaw in that person. Hating, the result of being a hater, is not exactly jealousy. The hater doesn't really want to be the person he or she hates, rather the hater wants to knock someone else down a notch."

That's a pretty good definition, if you ask me. I have a few thoughts about this. Prepare your toes because I'm about to step on them. Don't be surprised when you have "haters" if you are a "hater" to someone else. The reap what you sow principle applies to way more than just money.

So you have a hater. You have two or three haters. You have an army of them. Congratulations. I don't want to come across as someone who isn't understanding of your situation. This book is called *Chasing Better*, not *Chasing Pity Parties*.

I get it. You don't like it when others talk negatively about you. You don't like the fact that there are others sitting around thinking about how much they don't like you for whatever reason. Most people today are people pleasers. We do whatever we have to do in order to get people to like us, and we can't stand the thought of somebody out there that disapproves of our life. Seven billion people on the planet, and we get bent out of shape if a handful of them aren't fans.

If I'm honest, I am not a big fan of people thinking negatively about me either. If you ever want to know what its like to have a group of people not like you, try being a pastor for a little while. My goodness. As a pastor, you have to receive a direction for where you feel the church needs to go. You pray. You seek counsel. You implement change. Then you deal consistently with the ramifications of what happens when people don't like that change. I always thought it was funny that people in church wanted the pastor to "hear from God" and then strongly disapproved of it if it wasn't something they supported. I don't think this is true of all churchgoing people. It's just funny to me that in the eyes of many Christians, God's will looks a whole lot like whatever our preferences are.

Shots fired. The truth is, pastors aren't the only ones who deal with this. We all deal with this, especially if you are a leader. Jeremy DeWeerdt is the pastor of an awesome church in Rockford, Illinois, and one of my closest friends and mentors. I'm not sure if he is the one who originally said this or not, but I have heard him say it often, "Everyone loves you until you lead."

If you have any desire to be a leader at anything, dealing with criticism is just part of the territory. One of my favorite authors and motivational speakers is Grant Cardone. He talks often about how you should be grateful for haters. Be grateful for them because the only reason you have them is because someone knows who you are.

LESSONS FROM THE OLYMPICS

MY WIFE AND I ARE BIG FANS OF THE OLYMPICS. ALLOW ME TO CLARIFY. WE ARE BIG FANS of SOME of the Olympics. I am much more of a Summer Olympics guy than a Winter Olympics guy. Say what you want, but I love watching gymnastics and swimming. I'm not really into the track and field stuff. We love watching the opening ceremonies, cheering on the USA at whatever they are competing in, and trying to figure out exactly how curling works.

Michael Phelps has absolutely dominated the Olympics for the past decade. He is the most decorated Olympian in the history of the Olympics. He swam in five Olympics, winning twenty-eight medals in total with twenty-three of them gold.

Michael Phelps has a legendary work ethic. His preparation is crazy. He spends hours in the pool. Jumps from warmer water to colder water. Eats a ridiculous amount of calories because of the amount that he burns while swimming. He's a monster in all of the good kinds of ways. Is he perfect? Not even close. Neither am I. Neither are you. Whatever his imperfections in life may be, the guy flat out knows how to swim. Really, really fast.

Michael Phelps has haters, too. In the 2016 Rio Olympics, a swimmer from South Africa name Chad le Clos criticized Michael Phelps. In reality, the rivalry started before the Olympics, when le Clos shocked everyone by beating Phelps in the 200 meter butterfly swim at the 2012 games, which was one of Phelps's signature events.

Apparently, Phelps was cordial in defeat, and the two had mutual admiration for one another. A few years later, Phelps had gotten into some trouble with a DUI and wasn't allowed to swim at an event le Clos was swimming in while competing in the 100 meter butterfly. Le Clos put up a great time, and an interviewer asked him about his rivalry with Michael Phelps. He said:

"Michael Phelps has been talking about how slow the butterfly events have been recently, but I just did a time he hasn't done in four years. So, he can keep quiet now."

If there hadn't been a swimming rivalry before between the two, there was now. Phelps wasn't a fan of those comments. At the 2016 games, there was a picture that went viral of Phelps and le Clos just before they would compete against each other in the 200 meter butterfly event. In the picture, Phelps is giving the one death stare to rule them all in the direction of Chad le Clos.

The race starts, and Phelps has a commanding lead in the race. There is a picture of the event that shows both swimmers who are swimming side by side in this race with the whole world watching. Michael Phelps is in the lead, looking straight ahead, focused on the finish line. Chad le Clos is in second place, looking the entire time at Michael Phelps. Michael Phelps was focused on winning the gold medal. Chad le Clos was focused on beating Michael Phelps.

That picture has become a powerful statement for me. I use it as a screensaver on my computer. It's a powerful reminder to me for several reasons. Do I want to be the guy focused on winning? Or do I want to be the guy focused on the guy who's winning?

INFATUATION WITH CELEBRITY

I WANT TO BE THE GUY WHO'S FOCUSED ON WINNING. I HAVE FULLY COME TO UNDERSTAND that if you choose to focus your life on winning, people will be focused on you. We are funny people. Our fascination with celebrity in this country is well documented. We love our athletes and musicians and our Hollywood stars.

We are very quick to build them up, and we are equally quick to tear them down. We build them up because many people live vicariously through their favorite stars. We know what their favorite Starbucks drink is. Where they had dinner last night. What they named their children and who they are currently dating.

We can all become "fangirls" in a hurry around those who carry the title of fame. I don't want to get into the psychology of why we care so much about celebrity. I have a theory. I don't know if it's true. But it's my theory.

My theory is that the reason we are so infatuated with celebrity is because there isn't much else in our lives that we are excited about. We have stopped dreaming. We have stopped imagining what our life could become and instead have settled to watch with awe and a little bit of envy as people live the life that we wished we lived ourselves.

We build them up because we long to be them. We tear them down because we want them to be just like us.

I'm nowhere close to resembling a celebrity. I am about as average a guy as there ever could be. If you looked up "pasty white dude," in the Urban dictionary, you'll see a picture of me with a sunburn giving a dorky thumbs up. Maybe not, but I bet you want to go to Urban Dictionary right now to look up pasty white guy to see for yourself. You can admit it. I'm not judging.

I don't know if I have "haters" or not. I'm sure there are those out there who aren't fans of mine. There may be people who don't care much for me who are reading this book. They are looking for all the typos and trying to find places that I have misused to, too, and two somewhere in the book.

I'm sure I've been "unfriended" on Facebook and "blocked" on Instagram. Does that give me haters? Maybe. I can guarantee you one thing: I'm not focused on the people who aren't fans of who I am or what I do. I'm focused on the people who want my help. I have a motto that I try and live by. I am going to give my best to assist the ones who want my help, and I'm going to show love and grace to everyone else.

My former pastor, who just recently passed away, Sam Mayo, always told us, "You can't stop a bird from flying over your head, but you can stop it from building a nest in your hair."

He was so right. You can do nothing to control what other people say or think about you. You can try and be a good person. You can control your actions and your reactions. How they perceive them is completely up to them.

OUT OF CONTROL

STOP WORRYING ABOUT THINGS YOU CAN'T CONTROL. AND IF THERE IS ONE THING THAT WE definitely cannot control, it's other people talking negatively about us, whether to our faces or behind our backs. I've often had to ask myself, "Why does it bother me so badly when others say negative things about me? Why does that really matter? Why do I need everyone to like and approve of who I am and what I do?" I used to be so bothered by this. While I wouldn't say that I LOVE it if I find out others have been talking negatively about me, my attitude has shifted. I've gone from, "I can't believe they would say that," or "How dare they?" to "I'm glad my life is so interesting that you feel compelled to talk about it so often."

I truly mean that. If there is anyone in history who proves this theory true, it's Jesus. Jesus did so much good for so many people. He still had his critics, though. At least your critics aren't plotting to kill you. And if they are, stop reading this book right now and call the police.

Jesus' message was so offensive to His critics, the Pharisees, that they conspired to end His life. Jesus wasn't the first person to be killed because of a message He believed in strongly. Humanity has a tendency to react strongly when others don't share the same ideals that we do. We don't understand people who don't vote the way that we vote.

Look at the difference between Jesus and the Pharisees, and truthfully ask yourself which of these you want to be. The Pharisees heard words that Jesus was speaking. Jesus was intentionally calling them out. He wasn't talking behind their backs. He was telling them to their faces. He was exposing corruption and pride. The Pharisees didn't like it at all. So what did they do? They got defensive, and they eliminated a threat. At least, that is what they thought they were doing.

Jesus, on the other hand, spoke truth. Stood behind what He said. He wasn't passive aggressive. He didn't say one thing to one group of people and another to a different group. He was consistent with His message. Even after they beat Him senseless, He never wavered. People weren't just talking badly about Jesus; they were taking away His life. They didn't just take away His life. They took away His dignity. Publicly. Isn't that what we try so hard to protect? Our dignity? Our legacy? Our pride? How did Jesus respond to these people who took His life? With some of the last words He said, He found the strength to mutter, "Father, forgive them, for they know not what they do."

We shouldn't be worried that people are criticizing us. We should look at who is criticizing us. I want you to think back to the last time you knew beyond the shadow of a doubt that someone was talking badly about you. Who were they? What was their life like? Were they people that you want in your life? People who were positive and who made you better? Or were they people who drained you?

Don't be upset that people are critical of you. You should be happy if there is a segment of society who are critical of you. I hope that I repel some people. I hope that there are some people I annoy. I hope there are some people who get annoyed with this book and don't finish it. Don't do that. I've got some surprises later on you won't want to miss. ☺

HATER FUEL

IF YOU DESIRE TO BE SUCCESSFUL, YOU WILL HAVE HATERS. IT JUST COMES WITH THE TERRI-
tory. You have a choice to make in how you respond to haters. They can either be the thing that you use as an excuse or the thing you use as motivation. They can be the very thing that keeps you where you are or the thing that propels you forward. I have learned, however, that proving people wrong isn't always the best motivation.

Michael Phelps wasn't motivated to just beat Chad le Clos; he wanted to win the gold medal. If he happened to beat le Clos along the way, so be it. My motivation is never to prove somebody wrong. I don't want to give them that much power and influence over me. I'm not doing what I am doing to prove anyone wrong. I'm doing what I am doing because my reason is that important, and I refuse to allow anyone, anything, or a word that anyone says to me to stand in my way.

If you get crazy focused on a goal that you are trying to accomplish, don't be surprised when the negative voices that start to rise to the surface are those of friends and family. This is a tricky subject. We all know what it is like to have friends and family who are critical of what we do. I also want to say that, sometimes, we need our friends and family to be critical of us. Sometimes, we need to grow a backbone and stop throwing a fit when the people closest to us don't wholeheartedly support everything we do. Don't be a victim. They have a different opinion than you. That is ok.

I have, on multiple occasions, done dumb things that my friends and family told me were dumb, and I am grateful they cared enough about me to tell me the truth. I didn't always listen. I'm grateful that I have friends and family who tell me what they think, even if they know I won't always like it.

That being said, there are other times when I have had friends and family say some things that I didn't listen to. Intentionally. I wish I had a magic equation that could help you figure out how to differentiate between someone being critical and someone being concerned. I have learned, however, that just because someone is concerned about me doesn't mean I am in the wrong. I get one life to live. I intend to live it on my terms.

WHEN FRIENDS AND FAMILY BECOME THE OBSTACLE

I WAS READING AN OUTSTANDING BOOK BY STEVEN PRESSFIELD, CALLED *DO THE WORK*. IN it, he talks about how sometimes, friends and family can be the greatest obstacle that we have to overcome because their opinions of us carry more weight than someone we don't know. This is what he said that absolutely gripped me.

"The problem with friends and family is they know us as we are. They are invested in maintaining us as we are. The last thing we want is to remain as we are."

There is so much wow in that statement. Your friends and family know you as you are and love you that way. They tell you that often. But, many times, they want you to stay the way that they know you. But the last thing we want is to remain the same. We are chasing better. We aren't trying to be elitist. We aren't striving to be better than our friends and family. We are just striving to be better than WE WERE yesterday. Some people just don't want to take that same journey.

I was recently at an event in Las Vegas and heard a guy speak whom I had never heard of before. His name is Ed Mylett. He's a coach. Entrepreneur. Motivator. Pretty much an all-around stud. I HIGHLY suggest signing up for his podcast called, "Ed Mylett Show." It's free and incredibly motivating.

During his talk at the conference, Ed shared a metaphor. He compared our life to a movie. Once a movie is finished, the credits begin to roll. The stars of the movie are usually listed first. Jennifer Lawrence. Denzel Washington. Brad Pitt. Reese Witherspoon.

After the main actors or actresses are listed, the secondary characters are listed out. Every person who had anything to do with making this movie has their name listed on the credits. There are actors who don't even have a name in the movie who are listed. You get to see who played cab driver number 3.

Why is that significant? It's significant because your life is a movie. You are the main character in the story that is being written about you. When your movie is over, your name will be the first one listed when the credits roll. Each of us have secondary characters. Our family. Our friends. Our colleagues. You know what else every one of us will have in our movie? We all have cab driver number 3.

Here's what Ed said that completely rocked me. He said, "Why are you letting your life be negatively impacted because of what cab driver number 3 thinks about you?"

He doesn't even have a name in your story. He's an extra. She's not why people pay to see the movie. Never once have I walked out of a movie and thought, "That no-name cab driver NAILED it in that scene."

We all have cab driver number 3's in our lives. The question is, why do you allow them to take up so much of your headspace? Are they a main character? So what if they are critical? So what if they talk badly? So what if they unfriend me? They are cab driver number 3. They aren't horrible people. They have their own stories. But in my story? In my movie? They are cab driver number 3. I refuse to allow my life to be directed by the opinions of an extra.

CHAPTER 3

COACHING

"No one ever drowned in sweat."

—Lou Holtz

CONSTANT STATE OF LEARNING

I AM ONE OF THE MOST STUBBORN PEOPLE I HAVE EVER KNOWN. MY WIFE CAN ATTEST TO this. This can be a good trait. It can also be a very bad one. Stubborn is good when you are determined to succeed no matter what. It's bad when you refuse to change, no matter what. I wouldn't say I am a person who resists change. I'm actually incredibly impulsive. My wife is a careful planner. You can imagine this doesn't always mesh well. We certainly do balance each other out. There are also moments when my wife wants to throw things at me.

There is just something about us as people that likes to do things on our own without asking for help. Little kids do this all the time. Little kids want to do everything themselves. They want to eat by themselves. Tie their shoes all by themselves. Go to the bathroom all by themselves. We as adults can find this incredibly irritating, and, most of the time, we let them try before swooping in and just doing it ourselves because, quite frankly, it's just easier.

The problem with this strategy is, if we always do everything for our kids, they will never learn to do things on their own. Showing someone how to do something always takes time. Telling someone is easier. Doing it for them is easier still. People always learn best by being shown.

We show our kids how to tie their shoes. This is often an incredibly frustrating process. We show our kids how to do laundry. We show them how to make their own school lunches. We show them how to brush their teeth and put on deodorant and shave.

Kids are in a constant state of learning. Remember how many school subjects you had as a kid? Every day, you had math, science, history, foreign language, social studies, and physical education. At the end of each school semester, each one of those subjects had a final exam that accounted for a large percentage of your grade. You crammed like crazy.

Our brains are capable of retaining an incredible amount of information. We are capable of learning so much. That shouldn't stop the older we get.

Something happens to us after we graduate college and begin the process of settling down.

Think about this. Our culture pushes our kids so hard to be the best. We want them to have the best coaches and tutors. We want them to get great grades. We want them to earn scholarships. We wonder what percentile our young kids are in. How big their head is. How tall they are. How much they weigh. We constantly want to know how our kids stack up against other kids.

Once we get out of college, it's all about getting a job, a good job, a job with benefits and paid vacation that gives us the opportunity to exchange our time for money. Once we secure that job, it's time to get married and settle down. After we get married, it's time to have kids.

Isn't that the American dream now? We want our kids to get good grades in school so they can get a degree, find a good job, get married, and have kids. That's the life. I'm not knocking that life. I live that life.

WHY DO WE WANT TO SETTLE?

I DO WANT TO PUSH BACK A LITTLE ON THIS IDEA OF SETTLING DOWN. WHAT ARE WE SET-tling down for? I want you to think about this. Did you peak in high school and college? Is that when you were at your best? If you could live at any time in your life, would it be then? Or would it be now?

I truly believe that the season in life you are in right now should be the one that you are the most excited about living in. Are you driving the car of your life looking through the windshield at the possibilities of what could be, or are you living it looking through the rearview mirror looking at what was?

Think about this: If you were driving in your car and attempting to move the vehicle forward, where would your eyes be looking? You would be looking through the windshield, right? You only look through the rearview mirror if you are attempting to see what is behind you. If you want to move forward, you need to look forward. Your vehicle will always move in the direction your eyes tell it to.

If you were driving your car forward, but looking into the rearview mirror, how long would that be able to continue before you crashed into something? This is such a true metaphor for our life. We wonder why we keep crashing into things when the vast majority of our time is spent thinking about something that happened in the past. I don't care if it's dwelling on the good things or the bad things, dwelling there isn't a good idea. I once heard someone say, "The past is a great place to visit but a terrible place to live."

One of my good friends, Karen Schatzline, said, "Your past just called, and it had nothing new to say."

We consistently drift toward the past. Our eyes are just trained to keep looking in that rearview mirror. It's ok to remember. It's not ok to regret. It's ok to reminisce. It's not ok to constantly try and relive something that already happened.

Are your best days in front of you? Or are your best days behind you? I've put a lot of thought into this for my own life. I want you to join me in a fun little exercise. Don't be a rebel. Do this in the margins of this book or on a spare sheet of paper or the notes in your phone. I want you to write down the names of two or three of your favorite teachers or coaches that you have ever had in your life.

OUR FAVORITE COACHES

ONE OF MY FAVORITE COACHES WAS MY LITTLE LEAGUE BASEBALL COACH, TERRY WALKER. HE always believed for the best in me and wasn't afraid to call me out when my effort could have been better. I was never the best baseball player on our team. He did help me to become better and even make the all-star team all three years I played for him.

Mrs. Jenkins was my English teacher in high school. She taught me to love to write. I don't remember being good at very many subjects when I was in school. She encouraged me in my writing. Isn't it interesting that we tend to gravitate toward doing the things that people tell us we have a gift for? Why is that? I think it's because most people are sorely lacking in the encouragement from others category. Our emotional tanks are like our stomachs. Just because we eat once doesn't mean we are good for the week. One encouraging word is great. Just because I was encouraged yesterday doesn't mean I don't want to be again today.

Why is it that if I asked you who your favorite coaches or teachers were, you would most likely tell me someone who was in your life when you were young? Why did you think back to high school or college or even earlier? Do you want to know the reason?

The reason is because when we get older, we don't think we need teachers and coaches anymore. We think young people are the ones who need coaches and teachers. We think student athletes are the ones who need coaches. If I'm thirty-five and married with two kids and make 65k per year with three weeks of paid vacation and a mortgage, why do I need a coach?

This is what we tell ourselves. This is what I told myself. I don't need a coach. What would they even coach me for or about? Let's start with the basics. What is the purpose of a coach? What is the purpose of any coach?

Does the coach need to be better than the person they are coaching at whatever it is they are coaching them in? Obviously the answer to that question is no. Was Phil Jackson a better basketball player than Michael Jordan? Is Bill Belichick a better quarterback than Tom Brady? No.

The coach's job is to help their players perform at their highest level. We get tunnel vision. We have blind spots. We get stuck. A coach is there to push us toward things that we are afraid of or didn't think was possible. A good coach truly is worth a great deal. Tiger Woods has multiple coaches who help him tweak his golf swing constantly. A coach can see things in us that we cannot possibly see on our own.

Have you ever heard this quote before? "The definition of insanity is to do the same thing over and over again and expect different results."

If you are chasing better at anything in your life, I cannot recommend to you highly enough the importance of having a coach. You can call that coach whatever you want. A coach. A teacher. An accountability partner. A sensei. A pastor. A mentor.

I'm not trying to limit you. I'm not trying to tell you what you can't do. I just very much doubt that you will be all you could be in your life all by yourself. What is it that you want? Do you want to be in great shape? A coach can help you do that.

Do you want to learn how to be a better speaker? A better singer? A better dancer? Do you want to learn how to make more money? What is it that you want? Once you figure out what it is that you want, start thinking about people who have what you want.

How did those people get the very thing that I desire? What did they do? What do they know that I don't? You can either look at them with envy and remain the way you are or begin a relationship with them and find out what they know.

ELIMINATE THE EXCUSES

MOST PEOPLE WHO ARE SUCCESSFUL ARE MORE THAN WILLING TO TELL YOU HOW THEY became successful. If you find someone who looks amazing, ask them what they did to look that amazing. I guarantee you they will be willing to tell you. They won't be annoyed. They will be flattered. They worked very hard to look the way they look. They are just glad someone noticed.

If you want to be successful at anything, it's going to take a lot of work and bucket loads of sweat and determination. I'm not going to lie. I just threw up in my mouth a little bit writing that. But its true.

If you want something, you need to be willing to work for it. I can almost guarantee you that the person you envy for what they have worked incredibly hard to achieve it. They also almost certainly didn't acquire what they have on their own.

"But I don't have money to hire a coach."

First of all, if you want to move forward, you need to stop making excuses. Stop thinking about what you don't have and start asking what you do have. Not all coaches cost money. Get out of the scarcity mindset! Stop filtering everything through the filter of cost!

I know that can be challenging to hear. I'm sure that just made more of you upset. That's my goal. I want to make more and more people upset with each passing chapter. Don't worry. For those who stick this out to the end, I have a surprise for you in the last chapter. Also, don't skip to the last chapter. I know you—you little rebel. No shortcuts.

We have the ability to make things happen if we think they are important to us. We are also really good at coming up with excuses if it's not important to us. Is growing important to you? Is being better a priority? Do you think it's possible to get better at whatever that thing is on your own?

Four years ago, I was at a place in my health that wasn't the best. I was thirty-five. I was thirty pounds overweight. I had zero energy. I wasn't a very good dad. I wasn't a very good husband. I knew that I needed to make a change, but I had no clue what to do or how to do it. I had always been skinny. Now I was just skinny everywhere except my stomach. I had full-blown dad bod.

I was always blessed with pretty amazing metabolism. Growing up, I ate literally whatever I wanted to. I was full-blown addicted to Dr. Pepper, drinking at least four or five cans per day. No wonder I would want to fall asleep in my office every day at 2 o'clock.

I knew I needed to make a change. I just wasn't exactly sure what to do or how to do it. I heard about a friend of mine who had lost a bunch of weight. I decided to give him a call to see what he was doing and thought I would give it a try.

I found out that he was a coach who was now helping others lose weight and feel pretty amazing. I was thirty-five years old and was desperately in need of some help and accountability for my health, so I decided to get the help of a coach. Dan helped me not just change my health, but really change my life in so many ways.

THE STUDENT BECOMES THE TEACHER

WE NOW HAVE THE OPPORTUNITY TO PAY IT FORWARD TO HELP A LOT OF OTHER PEOPLE GET healthy just as we did. The student became the teacher. The apprentice became the master. Isn't it interesting that many professional sports coaches used to be players themselves for the sport they coach?

They love the game. They know the game. Father Time is truly undefeated. Tom Brady is like eighty-seven years old and still plays quarterback. Eventually, Father Time will overcome. This isn't meant to be depressing. Most coaches don't get paid millions of dollars. Most coaches don't coach because of financial gain. They coach for two reasons.

- To give back to the game or activity they love so much
- To invest into the life of someone else

Why would you not want to surround yourself with people who are passionate about helping you become better at something? It's one thing to have a coach. It's another thing to be coachable.

Can I have your permission to challenge you? Do you really want to get better? Are you interested in becoming the best you that you possibly can be? You aren't meant to be someone else. You are meant to be you. You are meant to be your best you.

You didn't peak in high school. Life doesn't have to steadily go downhill after we turn thirty. You can chase better. It first starts with a desire. I most likely don't know you. I don't know the circumstances that have brought you to the place where you are in life. I am sure you have had challenges. I am sure life hasn't always been fair. You've been mistreated. You've been talked about. You've been passed over for promotions in favor of someone less qualified. You've been hurt. You've been wounded. Join the club.

CHANGE YOUR STARS

I DON'T SAY THIS TO YOU TO BE INSENSITIVE. AGAIN, I DON'T KNOW WHAT IT IS LIKE TO BE you. You and I need to ask ourselves a very important question: Does life happen to us, or does life happen through us? Are you a victim that has no control over what is happening, or is there something you can do? I love the movie *A Knight's Tale.*

The late Heath Ledger plays William, who was not born into knighthood. He came from poverty. His father wanted to give him his best chance to succeed, so he gave him away to someone who could help give him a better life.

As a grown man, William desperately wants to learn how to be a knight and compete in jousting tournaments. The problem is that he doesn't have noble birth. William remembers something he asked his father as a young boy.

"Father, can a man change his stars?" I won't give away the movie if you haven't seen it. You will have to watch for yourself. Also, if you haven't yet seen the movie *A Knight's Tale*, WHERE HAVE YOU BEEN?

Can a person change their stars? Can we become more than we currently are? Do we have any control over our destiny, or are we helpless pawns in a cruel game?

You may not be able to control what happens to you. You can control whether or not you allow someone to come into your life to help you become better. Do you honestly want to be better at something? I really don't care what it is. Being better at anything starts with a desire. Nobody can give you that desire but you. You've got to want it. I tell myself that every single day. I have a post-it note taped to my desk at home that simply says, "How bad do you want it?"

How bad do you want to change? How bad do you want to get better? Is it a goal? Or is it a wish? Which of these describes you?

"I'd like to change. I'd like to get better. I just have no idea how to do it."

"That just seems like a lot of work."

"I don't think I could ever do that."

"I want to change. I need to change. I will do whatever it takes."

Which of these hypothetical people do you think has the best chance? Which one do you want to be? Find someone who can help you get whatever it is you desire. I'll never forget what my coach, Dan, told me when I asked him about his health journey. He told me how he lost weight. He asked if I wanted to join him. I told him I would try to do some things on my own. I was grateful for his time, but I thought I could do it on my own without his help. This is what he told me that forever changed the course of my life.

"If you could have done it on your own, you would have done it already."

He was right. I invited him to help me, and my whole life changed. I took a chance. I took a risk. I trusted someone else. Amazing things happen on the other side of a decision to take a risk. Do you want to make a change? If you could have done that on your own, you would have done it already. Make a call. Send an email. Make the investment into making yourself better. You won't regret it.

CHAPTER 4

READING

"A person who won't read has no advantage over one who can't read."

— Mark Twain

FIVE LOVE LANGUAGES

IT'S IMPOSSIBLE TO WRITE A BOOK CALLED *CHASING BETTER* WITHOUT DEVOTING A CHAPTER to discussing the importance of reading. You are reading this book because you desire to be more successful. You want to make more money. You want to have more influence. You want to make a bigger impact. The first step to accomplishing any of those things is making a commitment to learn.

Americans are busy. At least, we say we are. I can almost guarantee you that if you surveyed 1000 people, all from different walks of life, and asked them the question, "Are you busy?" 100 percent of them would say yes. Busy means different things for different people. We like to play the who is busier game with our family and friends.

"They think they are busy? They should try having kids."
"They think they are busy? They only have one kid."

"They think they are busy? They only have two kids."

Somehow, we make ourselves feel better by winning the busy award. We tell people how busy we are in hopes they will look at us and say admiringly, "I just don't know how you do it." When we hear people say that, we breathe in a deep sigh before saying, "Well, I just do the best I can, but thank you for noticing."

Most of us are words of affirmation type people. If you have never read the book *The Five Love Languages*, I highly recommend it. It talks about the five ways that people give and receive love.

1. Quality time
2. Words of affirmation
3. Physical touch
4. Giving gifts
5. Acts of service

Every guy I have ever met in my life is a words of affirmation person. Most girls are, too. We are skilled at directing conversations back toward bringing compliments in our general direction. I know I am. I'm not sure that's a good thing. It's just honest. I like for people to say nice things about me, and I find myself directing conversations toward things that will compliment me. It just comes second nature. My ego craves positive feedback. Yours does, too.

THE BUSY AWARD

WE WANT TO WIN THE BUSY AWARD. THE TRUTH IS, NO MATTER HOW BUSY WE ARE, THERE IS always someone busier. No matter how many plates we have to spin, there is always someone spinning more. You will never win the busiest person award. I'm sorry to break that to you. The truth is, we generally tend to make time for the things that we want to make time for. If something is important to us, we will find the time. If something isn't important, we won't. It really isn't that difficult. Reading isn't happening as much today as it did twenty years ago. We aren't busier now than we were twenty years ago. We just have more distractions.

According to an article in the *Telegraph* in May of 2015:

"The average person has five social media accounts and spends around 1 hour and 40 minutes browsing these networks every day, accounting for 28 percent of the total time spent on the Internet."

One hour and forty minutes browsing social media. And that is just the average. You know there are some people who spend zero time. That means there are others who are spending five or six hours or more per day browsing social media. Social media is a powerful tool. I use it every single day. I love connecting with friends, and, for entrepreneurs like me, it's a great and free way to grow your business and build your brand. I'm very PRO social media.

In June of 2016, *The New York Times* published an article about how much time we spend watching television. This includes watching movies, shows, Netflix, Hulu, and others.

On average, American adults are watching five hours and four minutes of television per day. The bulk of that — about four and a half hours of it — is live television, which is television watched when originally broadcast. Thirty minutes more comes via DVR.

So let me see if I have this straight. We are busy people. Plates spinning all over the place. Yet in the midst of our busyness, we still find time to spend almost seven hours combined watching TV and browsing social media. I realize that many of us are multitaskers, and we browse social media while watching TV. I think its safe to say that Americans are addicted to entertainment.

I remember growing up and not being able to fall asleep unless the television was on. Do you fall asleep watching TV? Browsing your phone? Looking at nothing? All of a sudden, you have lain in bed for hours, and you can't fall asleep. That used to be me.

I am not anti browsing social media. I am not anti TV. I have binge-watched TV shows before, too. Don't go burn your sixty-inch plasma. I'm not telling you to cancel your Netflix account necessarily.

I'm asking for all of us to be honest with ourselves. What if someone was following you without you knowing about it, and they were logging literally everything you did all day long? What if they published those findings the following day for everyone to see exactly what you did the day before. Creepy? Maybe.

Here's the point. I don't think we are as busy as we let on. "But, Corey, you don't even know me." You are most likely correct. I don't know you. You aren't reading a book called, "already arrived at better;" you are reading about "chasing better."

You aren't reading this book for someone to pat you on the back and tell you that you are amazing. You are amazing. But you don't need another person telling you that. You might be amazing, but you could be better. Just like every other person on the planet, the only person standing in the way of you becoming a better version of you, is you.

BUDGETING OUR TIME

HOW MUCH TIME PER DAY DO YOU SPEND IMPROVING YOURSELF? WHAT IS YOUR ROUTINE?

I encourage you right now to sit down and map out your next day. Don't map out the rest of this day because, more than likely, it's already half over. Map out tomorrow. What if we budgeted our time in the exact same way that we budget our money?

You could make an argument that time is more valuable than money, right? We can make more money, but we can't make more time. What is your day going to look like tomorrow? Map it out. I dare you. You don't have to be exact with this, unless you know beyond the shadow of a doubt that you will be in the bathroom tomorrow morning from 11:33-11:37. That's a long time to pee. Either that or you are finding out who number 2 works for. Can I say that? Moving on...

Are you budgeting any time for you to work on you? I once heard someone say that if you don't fill up the space on your calendar, someone else will fill that space up for you. We tend to be controlled by whatever the next emergency is. Sure, emergencies happen. We all need to be flexible. Sometimes our plans get thrown out the window. If we aren't setting aside time to read and grow ourselves, 99 times out of 100 it isn't because of an emergency; it's because we didn't plan it.

If we didn't plan it, it means we don't value it. Sometimes we need to give ourselves permission to be selfish. If you have had any sort of Christian upbringing, you have been taught that being selfish is bad. We all should be people who put the needs of others ahead of our own—sometimes.

When it comes to working on you, I think its ok to be selfish. When you work on you, it makes you a better you, which means you can better take care of the people in your life who matter the most to you. I don't think people choose not to read out of a fear of being selfish. I think we choose not to read because we'd just rather be doing something else.

Why is it that we don't feel selfish watching five hours of TV and browsing social media for ninety minutes a day, but finding time to read does make us feel selfish? Do you see how easy it is for us to justify? If you aren't setting aside time to work on you, that is a you issue. It's not because you are too busy. It's not because you don't have the time. It's because it is not a priority to you.

EMPLOYEE OR CEO

WOULD YOU RATHER BE AN EMPLOYEE OR A CEO? MAYBE YOU WANT THE LIFE OF A CEO, maybe you don't. Maybe I should ask the question this way: Would you rather be paid like an employee or paid like a CEO? Stupid question, right?

Jim Kwik says that the average CEO or executive reads four or five books every month. The average person reads less than two books in a single year! Can I ask you a favor? Refuse to be cynical and be passionate about accepting personal responsibility. The mindset of a victim would be:

"Well, if I had the time they had, I would read four or five books a month, too. They have everyone doing everything else for them, so of course they have that much time to read. I should be getting paid more than the CEO does because I work harder than they do. All they do is prop their feet up on their fancy desks overlooking their amazing views while I do all the work to make them successful."

Does that make anyone else cringe? No? Just me? I hate to break it to you, but if you have that mentality, not much will ever change for you. Is it possible for you to go from employee to CEO overnight? Not likely. Again, first of all, you have to ask yourself if you desire to be a CEO. Do you desire to be an executive? Do you desire to earn six figures? Seven figures? Eight figures?

Many people want the salary, but they don't want to pay the price required to earn a salary like that. The vast majority of CEOs and top-level executives have those positions because they either worked their way up from starting at the bottom, or they started the company themselves. Almost every leader has a starting-from-the-bottom story.

Apple was started in a garage. Colonel Sanders was sixty-two when he started selling fried chicken on the side of a road in Kentucky. My daughters have hundreds of Barbie Dolls. They were made by Mattel, which is a maker of children's toys. Mattel was a company that started in California in the early 1950's. They made picture frames. They made the decision to sell some furniture for doll houses, and, in 1959, they released the first-ever Barbie Doll.

What does that have to do with you? Begin now! It's not too late for you. Figure out what it is that you desire. If you can't define what that is, that is a good indication of why you are frustrated. Many people just simply don't want to be better. That's ok. This is your life. You get to live it however you want to. You don't have to be a CEO. You don't have to run a business. You don't have to make seven figures. Many people are perfectly content working nine to five, and I think that is great. I don't want to project what happiness and contentment should be for you.

You aren't less than because you don't desire to grow. You aren't less than because you don't want to advance in your profession or start a company or earn a lot of money. Here's my point: Don't complain about your status in life if you aren't doing what is in your control to change it.

There are many people who want to grow. They want to lead. They want to earn more. They just don't know how. Many have fallen into the victim mindset of thinking that everything happens to them and that some entity is holding them back from achieving the life that they rightfully deserve.

Maybe you deserve it. Maybe you don't. That's not for me to decide. If CEOs read four or five books a month, shouldn't that tell us something? What if we stopped playing the victim and started embracing being a student? Do you often criticize the leaders and CEOs of companies you have been a part of?

"Those people who run this place are complete morons."

That's good news for you, right? If they are morons, and you, of course, are a rocket scientist, how much better could you be if you were as committed to learning and being better as they are?

WHAT DO YOU HAVE?

WHAT IF WE STOPPED FOCUSING ON WHAT WE DIDN'T HAVE AND STARTED FOCUSING ON what we did? Other people may have more money than you. They may have more talent than you. They may have more connections than you. But they don't have more time than you. Time is the one resource that is equally available to all people. How you use it is completely up to you. Are you absolutely laser focused on bettering yourself and your situation? If the answer is yes, what are you doing about it?

Nobody is going to push you to the front of the line because you are owed it. You are going to have to push yourself there. You don't get there by being negative. You don't get there by whining. You don't get there by continuously focusing on what you don't have or how many people are conspiring to hold you back. You are in control. You may not be in control of everything. But you are in control of something. That something is you and your schedule. Control it.

THE IMPORTANCE OF JOURNALING

I RECENTLY STARTED A HABIT THAT TOOK ME THIRTY-SEVEN YEARS TO BEGIN. I RECENTLY started journaling. I don't know why I put this off for so long. I'm sure I had the same excuses everyone else has.

"I don't have the time."

"I have nothing to write."

"Journaling is for girls."

None of these things are true. I am amazed at my ability to justify not doing something I know that I should be doing. The honest reality is that I wasn't journaling because I didn't see the value in it. I was having lunch recently with a good friend of mine named Mark. Mark is an avid journaler. He journals about journaling. He has volumes and volumes of journals from previous years. I began to think about how amazing a resource that must be. Mark has years of thoughts and experience that one day his kids and grandkids will be able to comb through to learn more about their dad and grandfather.

I tend to be fairly impulsive as a person. I remember having lunch with Mark at a BJ's a few months ago and him asking me why I didn't journal. I had no good, legitimate reason. I told him that I would start the following day. I went to Office Depot, purchased a journal, and committed to writing in it ten minutes a day, every day. As a person, I am REALLY good at starting things. I have shelves full of half-read books. I was determined this would be different.

Every day, I write for ten or fifteen minutes. I write honestly. I write whatever is on my mind. I write about my frustrations, my successes, my dreams, and my failures. I swear in my journals. Is that allowed? Of course it is! It's your journal! It's truthfully been one of the most therapeutic things I have ever done for myself. Something positive happens when you get the complicated, jumbled mess out of your head and onto a piece of paper. Some people type. I prefer to write in my journal. I show it to NO ONE. My wife doesn't even read my journals. This is my world. My thoughts. My complicated mess.

I'm complicated. Don't look at me that way. You are complicated, too. We all are. Journaling very simply helps me come up with solutions. It gets me out of excuse-making Corey and helps me get focused on solutions Corey.

I am amazed at how much my outlook on life and problems changes when I give myself space to write. What should you write about? Whatever you want. Don't focus on grammar. Make all the run-on or fragmented sentences you want to. The grammar police will not have a key to your journal. It's filled with the glorious imperfections that make you, you.

GO TO SLEEP!

I USED TO BE AN ATROCIOUS SLEEPER. PART OF ME BLAMES LIVING ON THE EAST COAST. WHY does everything have to start so late? Part of me blames the Cubs. I mean, I have to stay up late and watch every game even if it goes eighteen innings, right?

For the longest time, I had the most difficult time going to sleep at night. My mind was constantly on overload. I'm always thinking about the next day. I'm always replaying events from the previous one.

I have never been a person who enjoys waking up early. I read stats that talk about successful people waking up at 4:00 a.m., and I can't begin to describe how much I don't want to do that. I'm not saying I never will. I just REALLY don't want to be a 4:00 a.m. riser.

I also have learned that if I don't get six or seven hours of good sleep a night, I absolutely drag the next day. I typically get up at 6:00, which means I need to be asleep by 11 every night. I try and make sure I am lying in bed no later than 10:30. I love waking up at 6 because the rest of my house wakes up at 7. This gives me 1 hour every morning to read, journal and plan my day and be fully present with my girls and their morning routine when they wake up at 7. I have noticed how much more energy they have and how much better their mood is when I endeavor to be fully present, excited and awake when I get them up instead of half asleep and dragging. This decision to get up early and work on me has completely changed the mood of our entire house every morning.

Why am I telling you all of this? I'm telling you this because I have learned that the discipline isn't found in waking up early. It takes discipline to go to bed early. Everyone is different. Find what works best for you.

I have a friend named Andy who is one of the most dedicated readers I have ever met. He reads about one or two books every week. In the morning, he reads a business type growth book. At night, he reads fiction books.

When I asked him why, he told me that there were all kinds of benefits to reading fiction. Reading fiction helps grow imagination. It helps develop empathy for people. It also helps you wind down for the day way better than Netflix.

I can't think of a single thing more responsible for people sleeping less today than Netflix. I like Netflix. I've said, "Just one more episode," more times than I care to admit.

We've all been there, right? It's 11 o'clock at night. You have to be up at 6:00 a.m. You just finished an episode of your latest show craze, and it leaves off with a cliffhanger. You COULD watch the next episode tomorrow or the following weekend.

You are so sucked into the show that you stay up way longer than you should. You wanted to be in bed by 11:00, and you were just going to watch one episode. Now it's 1:30 in the morning, and you've watched four. You wanted to wake up at 6 to work out, but sleep until 7:30 and wake up groggy, frustrated, and don't feel like being productive. But at least you know what happened on the season finale of *This is Us*.

I'm not knocking *This is Us*. I've never seen an episode. As I mentioned before, I've binge watched shows in the past. I've stopped doing that. In fact, I couldn't tell you the last show I have binge watched. I'm not better than you. I'm not more disciplined than you. A person who doesn't watch Netflix isn't superior over someone who does.

ENTERTAINMENT ADDICTION

I REALLY THINK IT ALL COMES DOWN TO WHAT YOU DESIRE. WHATEVER IT IS THAT YOU DESIRE the most will receive the majority of your time. Do you desire to grow more than you desire to be entertained? America has a few addictions that don't get talked about very often. I'll talk about one now and one in the next chapter. I've already made you mad talking about money. Why stop now, right?

We are addicted to entertainment. Adults aren't that different from children if you think about it. My daughters are ten and seven currently. If you are a parent, you have heard these words from your kids before, "I'm bored."

When you hear those words from your kids, you begin to flip out a little. Every parent has given a "when I was your age," speech to their kids.

"We didn't have video games."

"We played outside."

"We didn't have Skyzone."

"We didn't have a TV with 4,872 cartoon channels."

"We invented our own games."

Your kids will say the same things to their kids twenty years from now. The technology will just have advanced a little.

"We didn't have hovercrafts."

"We didn't have robots."

"Nobody lived on Mars when I was little."

We get frustrated when our kids tell us they are bored. We get frustrated when our kids watch hours upon hours upon hours of things on a screen. Our kids are spending more time on screens now by far than ever before. According to a BBC article from March of 2015:

"Children aged 5 to 16 spend an average of six and a half hours a day in front of a screen compared with around three hours in 1995, according to market research firm Childwise. Teenaged boys spend the longest, with an average of eight hours."

Don't kids just model whatever they see their parents doing? I'm not calling you a bad parent if your kids like screens. I'm not calling you a bad parent if your kids watch screens. My kids like screens. My kids use them, too. This doesn't have to be an all-or-nothing approach.

My point is calling a spade a spade. Most of us can't use the "I'm too busy to read" excuse. We choose not to. We aren't too busy.

Getting better always starts with taking personal responsibility to lead yourself at a high level. No matter what you are trying to get better at in life, reading will help you get better, faster. Why would we not want to get into the minds of people who know more than we do about something?

If you are someone who currently doesn't read at all or hasn't started the habit of journaling, I wanted to close this chapter by giving you a few practical tips to assist you in getting started. Again, this book is called *Chasing Better.* I don't know one person on planet earth who could honestly say, "I have nothing in life left to learn."

If we want to move forward in life, we need to get out of the mindset of all or nothing and embrace the idea of getting better today than I was yesterday. If you hardly ever read, or never journal, how can that get better starting today?

Here are some practical tips on journaling.

1. Turn your phone onto Do Not Disturb.
2. Listen to instrumental music from a soundtrack.
3. Set a timer on your phone for how long you want to write and don't stop until the timer goes off. Start with ten minutes, and go from there.
4. I HIGHLY recommend getting a pen and actual paper to write on. Journaling on a computer or phone is certainly better than not journaling at all. There is just something about writing with a pen that helps creativity flow.
5. Just keep writing. Don't think. Just write. Write whatever is on your mind. Don't worry about someone reading what you write. Be honest. Be raw. Be you. Be consistent.

Here are some tips on reading.

1. Don't listen to music. It makes it very hard to concentrate on the words you are reading if there are other words you are listening to.

2. Find someplace quiet. Try not to read while the TV is on. You won't be focused.

3. Set a time that you want to spend reading every day and stick to it. Start with fifteen minutes. If you read for fifteen minutes a day, every day, you should be able to get through about two books every single month.

4. Use Audible and listen to books at 1.5 speed. It's fast enough so that you can get through books at a good pace while not being so fast that you can't comprehend at all what the person is saying.

5. Find a few people that you find inspiring, and see if they offer free podcasts. Most podcasts are anywhere from thirty to sixty minutes long and are great ways to learn or be inspired

For a full list of books and podcast recommendations, check out the appendix at the end of the book.

CHAPTER 5

MONEY

"Lack of money is the root of all evil."

—George Bernard Shaw

WORST JOB EVER

I DELIBERATED FOR QUITE SOME TIME BEFORE DECIDING WHETHER OR NOT TO USE THE above quote from George Bernard Shaw at the beginning of this chapter. To be truthfully honest, I don't know much about him. I don't know what he stood for or believed in. I'm not a believer in the idea that I need to know everything about a person before I can take something they say and learn from it. I believe I can learn from anyone.

I'm also fully aware that this quote is a spin-off of a verse in the Bible that says the "love" of money is the root of all evil. What if both of these statements could still be true? What if the very reason we love money is because we lack it? This chapter started hot and heavy, didn't it?

I grew up in a very small town in Northern Illinois called Rochelle. We were called the Rochelle Hubs. Our mascot was literally a wheel hub, because apparently our city of 10,000 people was the "hub" of a bunch of "small towns" surrounding it. Lame. I know. You should have seen our mascot. It was REALLY tough to use the restroom if you were wearing the wheel hub mascot costume.

My parents are two of the most amazing people I know. They both work incredibly hard. They raised four boys. Their kids are their life. I have never one time in my life felt like I wasn't a priority to them. We did not grow up wealthy. We got by just fine. I always had basketball shoes. We never went hungry. We took family vacations. We got Christmas presents. We lived in a nice house.

My parents would be the first to admit to you that it wasn't always easy. I'm sure that my brothers and I don't have any idea the sacrifices they made in order to help us get by during some challenging years. I remember getting my first jobs when I was twelve years old. I delivered newspapers. I detassled corn. If you have never detassled corn before in your life, consider yourself to be the luckiest person to ever walk the face of the Earth. No disrespect to Joe DiMaggio.

One of the first jobs I had was keeping score at the local bowling alley called Chelle Crest lanes. The bowling alley didn't have automatic scoring machines. They had transparencies. Someone had to actually keep score. None of the teams wanted to keep their own score, so they paid me to do it. I learned to do math pretty fast, and I also got paid $10 per night. I thought I was the richest kid at Rochelle Township High School because I earned $30 each week keeping score for bowlers. I also got free practice, which I'm sure kept me out of a lot of trouble. While other kids were going to parties and cruising the square in downtown Rochelle, I was hanging out at a bowling alley.

I am incredibly grateful that I learned to work at that age. I have always known that if there was something I wanted in life, I needed to work for it. I worked three jobs every summer in order to pay for college. I've paid my dues with garbage cars. One of my cars had a cracked man-ifold, which meant that the exhaust of the car came through the vents inside the vehicle instead of the exhaust pipe. Probably not the best to be inhaling exhaust while you drive.

Another one of my first vehicles was a four-door dodge 600. The only door that worked was the right rear one. In order to get into my car, I had to open the right rear door and climb over the seat. This was not exactly the most ideal car to take on a date. Fortunately, I didn't exactly date much in high school and college. Bowlers aren't known for savoir faire.

WHAT IS YOUR BACKSTORY?

MY WIFE JULIE AND I WENT THROUGH SOME CHALLENGING FINANCIAL TIMES FOR THE FIRST ten years of our marriage. We didn't get into pastoring for the money. We had our needs met. We made it through. Our congregation was EXTREMELY generous to us. Just like most of America, we lived completely paycheck to paycheck.

We've lost a house to a short sale. We've had to pay thousands for medical bills because the birth of our second child wasn't covered somehow under our "insurance." While I was pastoring, I donated plasma two days a week in my mid thirties for $300 a month. I remember feeling like garbage every time I went. I did it because we wanted to fly home for Christmas that year and didn't have the extra resources to make that happen without putting it on credit.

Why am I telling you all of this? I'm guessing my backstory isn't exactly riveting to you. I'm also guessing that you have your own backstory. Most of us do. We all know what it is like to struggle. We all know what it is like to have financial stress. If you are married, you have probably gotten into an argument or thirty about the subject of money.

I've learned that money stress is kind of like what happens when you get into a high altitude and have trouble breathing. When NFL teams travel to Denver, it's not uncommon to see players from opposing teams on the sidelines with oxygen tanks, just trying to get oxygen back into their lungs after being on the field for an extended period of time. If you aren't use to the high altitude, it can take your breath away very quickly.

Lack of money or financial stress can do that to us. It feels heavy. It feels like there is a big weight on your chest that just won't go away. Dave

Ramsey talks a lot about Murphy's Law. Murphy's Law is, "Anything that can go wrong will go wrong." Dave says this happens especially when you have no money. I wholeheartedly agree.

You've probably said, "What else is new?" a few times when you've been hit with an unexpected financial setback. It's so easy to get cynical when it comes to money.

There are many experts on this subject, and I certainly don't qualify as one of those. I'm just a guy. I'm a guy who has been broke. I'm a guy who has been in a lot of debt. I'm a guy who has worried a lot about money. I'm a guy who has lost sleep about money and fought with my spouse about money. I don't have all of the answers. I do have a few theories. I'm grateful to say that our financial situation today looks night and day better than it did even four years ago.

FINANCIAL GOALS

I TRULY BELIEVE THAT THE FIRST STEP TO IMPROVING YOUR FINANCIAL LIFE IS TO SET A GOAL. Not just any goal. Set a specific goal. Generic goals get generic results, and specific goals get specific results.

What are your financial goals? To be not broke? Take a three-month-long cruise of the Greek Islands? Buy your own Greek Island? What is it?

I have learned that, generally, people don't have what they desire financially for one of two reasons.

1. They don't know what they want.
2. They don't believe what they want is possible.

Bottom line: If you can't identify what it is that you desire, you won't put in the action necessary to accomplish it. If you don't believe what you want is even possible, then why bother putting in the action to accomplish whatever that is?

One of the best things I ever did was give myself permission to dream. I know that seems like a strange thing. I also gave myself permission to not be scared by money anymore. Christians can be funny about money.

Can I be completely transparent with you? I want to make a lot of money. I want to give a lot of money away. One of my lifelong goals is to write a check for a cause I care deeply about for one million dollars. You know what I have realized? I can't give away a million dollars if I don't have a million dollars.

As I mentioned before, I used to be a pastor. I'm truly grateful for those years and believe that shaped who I am today. One of the reasons I am no longer pastoring is because I felt like I wanted to pursue being an entrepreneur. I wanted to help people identify what their problems were and offer a solution to them. I've learned that really is the way to create wealth. Help someone identify their problem. Help offer a solution to that problem. Our society has lots of problems. We need more people willing to come up with solutions. I've also learned that if you can help someone create a solution to something they desire, which fixes a problem they have, they will be willing to pay for it. When that happens, they don't feel like you have sold them anything because they got what they wanted!

I just recently purchased a new car. I love it! I didn't drive away from the dealership offended that the dealer sold me something. I drove away thrilled because I got what I desired. I willingly exchanged money for something I desired. I know that is simple. That's the way our economy works. Find something that other people want. My wife and I realized several years ago that people want to be healthy. We help people be healthy. We help them create the lifestyle that they desire.

The more people you help, the more problems you help solve, the more you get compensated.

A devil's advocate could say, "If all you wanted to do was help people solve problems, why didn't you just continue to be a pastor?"

That is such a great question, and I am glad that you asked. Ready for some honesty? I want to help a lot of people. I want to make a lot of money. I want to give away a lot. People are uncomfortable with pastors making a lot of money. I definitely understand the reason behind this. Pastors don't pastor to make a lot of money. At least, they shouldn't do it for that reason. I want to make a lot of money. Does that make me a bad person? Maybe. I don't believe so, though. I think it makes me a normal person. At the very least an honest one.

YOU DRIVE A WHAT?

SEVERAL MONTHS AGO, I WAS AT A NETWORKING EVENT FOR ENTREPRENEURS, AND I BEGAN a conversation with a guy who is a financial planner. He helps people invest money into the stock market. He drives a Porsche. We got into a conversation and started talking about what we each did, and I told him I am a coach who helps people be healthy and that I am an author.

I also told him that I used to be a vocational pastor for eighteen years. He asked me why I left, and I told him that I wanted to be an entrepreneur and that I had a desire to create generational wealth so that I could help a lot of people. He got a small grin on his face.

The gentleman went on to say that it was interesting that I used to be a pastor and that he and his family go to a church in town that they had recently left. When I asked him why they had left, he told me it was because the pastor and his wife both drove a Mercedes and that he didn't want to belong to a church where the pastor drove a Mercedes.

I told this gentleman, "So, let me get this straight, you can drive a Porsche, but your pastor can't drive a Mercedes? Why is that?"

He went on to say that he didn't want all of his money going to purchase a nice vehicle for the pastor. I understand that. I also think it's a giant double standard. Let's be honest. We are uncomfortable with our pastors and church leaders driving nice vehicles and having lavish things.

Is there wisdom in this? Of course there is. Have some pastors and church leaders taken advantage of people? My goodness yes. Should there be checks and balances and boards and accountability? Without a doubt.

THE DANGER OF COMPARISON

I DON'T THINK THIS JUST RELATES TO PEOPLE WHO ARE IN MINISTRY. I THINK WE AS PEOPLE generally are uncomfortable with someone having more than we have or making more than we make. Have you ever noticed that we as people always compare ourselves to people who make more than we do? If I asked you what rich is, I can almost guarantee that you would say that rich is someone who makes about twenty-five to thirty thousand dollars more than you. You aren't rich. They are, though. Are you mad at me yet? Keep reading. It's about to get worse.

I want you to ask yourself a very honest question. What is your opinion of people who make more money than you do? Do you look up to them? Are they greedy? Would you use your money for so much more good than they do? I was always amused by people who said they would be generous if they won the lottery. Stop lying. You've done that, too. You have imagined winning the lottery and imagined all you could do with it. I think that's a normal thing. If I had more money, I would be so much more generous. I can't be generous now, but man I would be if I made 100k more than I currently am. Did you know that right now, there is someone looking at your lifestyle saying the exact same thing? That's because you make more than them.

What if we stopped comparing ourselves to people who make more or less than we do? You aren't better than people that make less money than you, and you aren't worse than those who make more. Contrary to what we sometimes think, God doesn't prefer us, nor does He prefer them. We have made money personal, and it shouldn't be that way. Money for us is a way to classify and compare. It's a way to elevate ourselves by demeaning someone else.

What if we stopped being afraid of money? What if we stopped being envious of those who have what we want? What if, instead of being critical of those who are successful, we used that as a motivator. If they can do it, why can't we? What if we stopped asking why others get to have what we don't and started asking, "How did they do it?"

SCARCITY

I TRUTHFULLY BELIEVE THAT ONE OF THE BIGGEST PROBLEMS WE HAVE AS PEOPLE AS THAT too often we operate with a spirit of scarcity. I listened to a podcast by

Rob Bell recently about this topic. Some people like Rob Bell. Some people don't. I happen to learn a lot from him. I think you can learn a lot from anyone. Did you know it was possible for us to learn from people with whom we don't agree? Did you know that people who have completely different theological views than you do can still teach you some things and help you be better? Shots fired.

In the podcast, Rob was talking about scarcity and how many people believe that the world is like one giant piece of pie. If someone else has a big slice of pie, it hinders my potential to have more because there is only so much pie to go around.

The success of someone else does not limit the possibility of success for you. If you believe in God, I want you to ask yourself a very simple question. Can God bless you while at the same time blessing someone else? Think about that. Why do we get so bent out of shape when someone else experiences abundance in their life? Do you honestly believe their success is a threat to your success?

I truly believe that if we want to win with money, if we want to "chase better" at how we handle money, it starts with changing the way we think about money. It starts with giving yourself permission to be successful. It starts with refusing to operate out of a spirit of scarcity. If you operate with a spirit of scarcity, you will find yourself constantly being bitter. Scarcity mindset people aren't a ton of fun to be around. I honestly believe that those who have a spirit of scarcity are more selfish than those who have millions of dollars. For the record, it is possible to have millions of dollars and still operate out of scarcity.

When a person operates out of scarcity, everything always comes back to them. They are upset because they don't have what someone else has. They believe the person who has more than they do is greedy and self-centered. Yet it's the person with the scarcity mindset who is constantly thinking about themselves and what they don't have. Angry with me yet? It's ok. I understand this is a sensitive subject. Can you change how much money someone else has or what they do with it? Is it doing you any good to silently judge everything they do or buy?

The obvious answer is no. What if you stopped using the energy it is taking for you to be bitter and jealous and started using it to create something new for yourself? It's way easier to be the armchair quarterback. It's easier to judge. Life is too short for that, though. You may not be able to change what someone else does with their money. You can change what you do with yours. Stop living vicariously through someone else. It's making you miserable. I truthfully believe it takes way more energy to be critical than it does to create. The problem is, we don't want to take personal responsibility. I love this quote by Joe Polish:

"Life has a way of giving to the givers and taking from the takers."

GOING TO SCHOOL

AS I STATED EARLIER, I DON'T CONSIDER MYSELF AN EXPERT ON ALL THINGS FINANCIAL. I CAN tell you that over the course of the last year, I have read over twenty books on the subject of money. Does that make me an expert? No. It does make me better than I was a year ago, though. I have read a lot of stuff from a wide variety of different authors and have learned something from each, even if they have differing viewpoints. I've learned from Dave Ramsey. I've learned from Grant Cardone. I've learned from Tony Robbins and Jen Sincero and Ed Mylett and Robert Kiyosaki.

If there has ever been a book that has completely transformed the way I view money, it would have to be *Rich Dad, Poor Dad* by Robert Kiyosaki. If you have never read *Rich Dad, Poor Dad*, make that the next book you read—after you finish this one, of course. ☺

In *Rich Dad, Poor Dad*, Kiyosaki talks about two men who had influence in his life regarding money. One was rich dad. One was poor dad. He says that money is very simple and that we can use it to purchase one of two things. We can purchase assets. Or we can purchase liabilities. Assets put money into your pocket. Liabilities take money out of your pocket. Liabilities are part of life. We all have taxes and housing and food and gasoline and clothes to buy.

This concept changed everything for me regarding money. We simply started spending money on things that put money into our pocket as much as we possibly could. I realize this takes time. I also realize that every person can start somewhere when it comes to investing. Is this going to take discipline? You bet your sweet bippy it will. I don't even know what a sweet bippy is, but it felt like it fit here.

One of the most important lessons I have ever had to learn was never to be willing to trade what you want most for what you want right now. What do we want now? We want stuff. What do we want most? We want financial freedom. Financial freedom comes from purchasing things that put money into your pocket instead of purchasing things that take money out of it.

Can I have your permission to shoot straight with you? Stop making excuses. They aren't getting you anywhere. You could argue excuses are actually setting you further back.

"Well, that's easy for you to say, Corey."

"But you just don't understand my situation."

"But I have bills."

"Everything is just too expensive."

"I don't even know where to start."

Keep saying statements like that, and you will continue to struggle financially for the rest of your life. There are 1,000 people who have said the following quote, so I really don't know who to give credit to. I didn't come up with this saying, but I endorse it 100%:

"If it's important, you will find a way. If it's not, you will find an excuse."

When it comes to money, when it comes to financial freedom, are you finding a way? Or are you finding an excuse? There is no magic pill here. Financial freedom can take years. Sometimes it can even take decades. The point is, are you getting better? Has your financial situation improved over the last ten years? If not, why?

Your life will become the direct result of the actions you take or the excuses you make. Which will it be?

THE NUMBER ONE FINANCIAL PROBLEM

WHAT IS GOING TO CHANGE SO THAT THE NEXT TEN YEARS OF YOUR LIFE LOOK DIFFERENT

than the previous ten? I want you to do an exercise with me. This will be fun, I promise. How much more money would you need per year in order for you to feel like you were secure financially? $25,000? $50,000? $100,000?

What is the likelihood that you go into your boss's office this week and he or she says to you, "You have been doing such a fantastic job for this company over the last decade that we have decided to give you a $50k per year raise. Go see Mary Jean in HR, and she will handle the paperwork."

Wouldn't that be an amazing day? How realistic is that? You may get a 3% cost of living raise every year or so. Is that cost of living raise going to get you further ahead? Dave Ramsey talks about learning to live on less than we make. That means a person who makes 100k per year and spends 100k per year is just as broke as someone who makes 30k per year while spending 30k per year. The person who makes 100k per year, according to Dave, is just broke at a higher level. He's right.

Dave Ramsey's books are a great resource to help people get out of debt. I have learned a lot about money from reading his books. While I don't agree with everything he teaches about the subject of money, I can still say that he has been instrumental in helping our family get into a much healthier financial place than we were five years ago.

Where he and I differ is Dave talks about the biggest priority for a family being to get out of debt. While I agree in theory that getting out of debt should be a big priority, I don't think that is our major problem. We do have a spending problem in this country. Most people have next to no money set aside for emergencies. We live paycheck to paycheck and are just one major financial setback away from complete disaster. Get out of debt. Learn to have discipline when it comes to spending money.

I think our biggest problem is that we don't bring in enough income. We have an earning problem. Allow me to balance this statement, as

I'm sure, by now, I have several people getting ready to throw this book across the room in disgust. Stick with me. If you think you are upset now, just keep reading.

Most people don't make enough money. You can get out of debt all you want. You can have discipline all you want But until you address how much money you are bringing into your house, money will always be an issue for you. All of these things work together. Should we get out of consumer debt? Yes. I'm not anti-credit card. I use them like crazy. I'm just disciplined enough to pay the balance of them off each month. My family purchased annual Disney passes this year with credit card points. Take that, Dave Ramsey. I kid, I kid. I know credit cards CAN get people into trouble just like the Internet CAN get people into trouble. Just because something has the potential to be bad doesn't mean it always has to be that way.

Get out of debt. Learn to have discipline when it comes to spending. Learn to figure out what is a want and what is a need. All wants aren't bad. Having a want doesn't make you bad. It makes you human. We all have wants, and you shouldn't feel bad for wanting things. You just have to decide what it is that you want most. Spend your money on whatever that is.

Do you want to get out of debt? Spend your excess money on getting out of debt. Many of us don't know what excess money even is. That may mean it's time for you to downsize. Sell some stuff. Cut the cable. Downgrade your cell phone plan. Drive for Uber. Start a work-from-home side hustle business on the side. Do something to create financial margin in your life.

I am a huge fan of board games. If you want to play a game that will teach you a TON about money, I highly recommend purchasing a board game called Cash Flow. It was created by Robert Kiyosaki and helps a person learn about investing and how to use it to get out of the financial rat race. What is the financial rat race? Go to work. Get paid. Pay bills. Rinse, repeat.

DREAM BOARDS

ONE OF THE BEST EXERCISES MY WIFE AND I DID WHEN IT CAME TO HELPING US GET OUT OF the financial rat race was create a dream board. I realized that we really had no clue about what we wanted. We created a board. With pictures. I already told you a few things on our dream board. Allow me to tell you a few more.

1. Purchase our dream home with a bowling alley in the basement

2. Have vacation homes in Chicago and Orlando

3. Cubs season tickets

4. Give away a million dollars to a cause we care about

5. Twenty investment properties paid for in cash

6. European cruise

7. Take our kids to all fifty states

What is on your dream board? If you don't have one, make one. Make it visual. Put it in a place that you have to see it every single day. Again, many people don't have what they want because they can't identify what they want. Identify what you desire. The second reason people don't have what they want is they don't believe it's possible. I believe every single one of these things is possible. We may not achieve them in the next twelve months. But they are possible.

Identify what you want. Put a plan in place to make it happen. Focus on what you do have instead of what you don't have. You may not have a lot of money. Do you have time to learn? Can you fill your mind with knowledge from experts? Do you not have money for books or ebooks? Get a library card. There are also THOUSANDS of completely FREE podcasts about money. Please. Stop. Making. Excuses.

Stop focusing on what you can't do. Stop focusing on what is going wrong. What is in your hands right now? Build on that. Do you really want financial freedom? What is financial freedom? The ability to do what you want, when you want. Do you have that? If the answer is no, do you desire it? If the answer to that question is yes, chase it like something is chasing you.

Your obsession will eventually become your reality. The problem is we obsess over the wrong things. We obsess about what will happen when things inevitably go wrong and not about what life will be like if we put in the actions necessary to create that life. Stop saying, "what else is new." Stop saying, "Here we go again." Stop saying, "Now what." Quit it. Knock it off. You are obsessing about negativity and it is getting you nowhere.

Financial freedom gives you the ability to do some pretty amazing things. You can help a lot of people with financial freedom. I don't say this to brag or toot my own horn. I'm currently at Starbucks, and a group of Marines just came in to purchase breakfast and coffee. When they got up to the register, I went up and gave my credit card to the barista and told them I am buying whatever it is that they want. The Marines were grateful. They are the heroes. Not me. I paid a few dollars for a person's breakfast. They risk their life.

The barista behind the counter started crying when I did that. She told me how she wants to be able to do that for people someday. I told her she absolutely can. Financial freedom isn't just about what you can do for yourself. It's about what you can do for others. Generosity simply moves the needle. I want to inspire people with my generosity. How about you? Chase after financial freedom, and watch and see how many lives you will be able to impact as a result.

CHAPTER 6

HEALTH

"True healthcare reform starts in your kitchen, not in Washington."

—Anonymous

WHO IS THAT GUY?

I'LL NEVER FORGET THE DAY MY DAUGHTER CAME HOME FROM SCHOOL EXCITED TO SHOW ME a picture that she had drawn in class that day. My daughter Addison had just started first grade, and they had been asked in class to draw a picture of what their family does at night. Addison drew a picture of herself and her sister (Sadie) playing Barbies. She drew a picture of her mom in the kitchen with a fancy apron making dinner. She then drew a picture of what I can best describe as a blob on a couch.

I asked Addison what that was. "That's you!" she exclaimed proudly. I needed some clarification. She was six at the time, so I really wanted to be careful to celebrate her creativity while at the same time get some answers as to why I looked like Jabba the Hut in her latest drawing. She went on to tell me that she had drawn a picture of me, sitting on a couch, with my cell phone in my hand. When my daughter was asked to describe her family, she thought of me sitting on a couch playing on my cell phone.

I was crushed. I didn't want to be that guy. How had I turned into that guy? How had I turned into the guy who came home from work completely and utterly exhausted without the energy sufficient to spend time with the ones who mattered most to me?

I was pastoring at the time. My eating habits were terrible. I ate out every single day. I drank four or five cans of Dr. Pepper every single day. I had an enormous gut. I had zero energy. I didn't really know what to do, but, more importantly, I didn't really have a desire to change.

I needed a wakeup call. Your daughter basically calling you a lazy slob in a drawing has a way of doing that. As I mentioned in the previous chapter, I made a phone call one day that changed my life. I called a friend of mine who had lost a ton of weight and asked him for some help to do the same. Not only did I lose thirty pounds, I learned some amazing habits along the way, and I'm proud to say that I am now thirty-eight years old and have more energy, more muscle, more confidence, and even look younger than I did at twenty-eight.

Let me tell you first what this chapter won't be about. I'm not going to tell you how I lost weight. I'm not going to give you ten easy steps. I'm not going to send you to some website. Here's what I know: If you truly want to eat better or build muscle or both, there are tons of ways to accomplish that. I truly believe that if you want to be healthy, you will figure out a way.

I know there is a tremendous amount of opinion about this topic. Let me also say that I fully understand that many people deal with things related to their health that are outside of their control. They truly desire to be healthy. They didn't choose the disease they have. I completely get that. These words are meant for people who CAN change the course of their life and health by choosing to implement healthier habits.

I'm also not a health expert. I don't have a nutrition degree. I don't have a cooking show. I'm not a food scientist. I'm just a guy with an experience. I haven't talked about faith a ton in this book, but, as a former minister, it has obviously been a part of my life. I don't think it's my responsibility to tell you how to think or what to believe. I'm just sharing my experience.

EXPERIENCE VS ARGUMENT

THERE IS A STORY IN THE BIBLE ABOUT A MAN WHO HAD BEEN BORN BLIND. HE WAS NOW AN adult and came to see Jesus. Here's where it starts to get a little strange. Jesus looks at this man, spits on the dirt to make some mud, and rubs the mud on the dudes eyes. Awkward.

Jesus tells him to go to the river to wash out the mud, and, after he does, his sight is restored. For the first time in his life, he can see. Jesus has some critics called the Pharisees. They were religious leaders who were threatened by Jesus because He taught things they didn't agree with.

Trying to prove that Jesus was a fraud, they questioned the man who had been healed, along with his parents. The parents wanted zero part of talking to these guys and basically threw their son under the bus. The Pharisees asked the parents, "This is your kid, right? And he was born blind?"

They responded, "Yeah, that's our kid. Yeah, he was born blind. Yeah, he can see now. We don't know how that happened. He's old enough to speak for himself. Ask him." Exit stage right.

By this time, the former blind man was annoyed. He honestly didn't know a whole lot about Jesus. He knew who He was, but didn't know much about Him. After being consistently questioned by the Pharisees about who Jesus was or whether or not He was a sinner, the young man responded,

"Whether he is a sinner or not, I don't know. One thing I do know. I was blind but now I see!" John 9:25 (NIV)

Have you ever heard of the song "Amazing Grace" before? I'm guessing you have.

"Amazing Grace, How sweet the sound That saved a wretch like me I once was lost, but now am found T'was blind but now I see"

This is a chapter about health, right? Why is this dude quoting the Bible and singing famous hymns when talking about health and nutrition? Stick with me. I feel a lot like that blind man. Yes, I do feel grateful and awakened. Yes, I do think that I walked around blind as to the effects of a poor diet for a long time. That's not why I can relate to this man.

I relate to this man because when asked whether Jesus was a sinner or not, his honest assessment was a profound, "I don't know." I love that answer. I use that answer often when people ask me questions. I think people want honesty more than they want expertise. One of my favorite quotes is, "A person with an experience is never at the mercy of a person with an argument."

Most everyone has an opinion about health. Doctors can't even agree about what is good for you and what is bad for you. Chicken is good; chicken is bad. Milk is good; milk is bad. Don't have gluten. You can have a little gluten. Is there anything that DOESN'T have gluten? What in the world is gluten?

It's not just experts who have opinions about what is healthy and what is not. I think we know that deep fried Twinkies probably aren't the best for us. I'm sure we all can agree that we should probably eat more vegetables than we currently do. We all know that we should drink more water and less soda. We also know that knowing something and doing something about it are two different things entirely.

I'm not going to spend a lot of time telling you how to get healthy. I want to talk about why that is important. I truly believe that if you can figure out why you want to be healthy, the how will take care of itself. I've heard it said that losing weight or eating healthily is actually pretty easy. It's convincing our mind that is the hard part.

WHAT DO YOU DESIRE MOST?

THIS ISN'T MEANT TO SCARE YOU. TRUTHFULLY, FEAR ISN'T THAT GREAT A MOTIVATOR. YOU aren't a bad person because you crave ice cream and deep dish pizza. That makes you a normal person. Here is the secret to being healthy: Find out what it is that you desire more than the food that you are craving.

We need to learn how to never be willing to trade what we want now for what we want most. What we want now is to fulfill a craving. What we want most is optimal health and a long, active, and productive life. The next time you are craving something you know you shouldn't be eating, stop and ask yourself if there is anything in the world you desire more than the thing you are currently craving.

Think about the thing you crave the most when you walk into a gas station. It's something different for all of us. There aren't a lot of healthy options in gas stations. Let's play "Let's make a Deal." Remember that show? There is something behind door number one and something else behind door number two?

Let's say you walk into a gas station absolutely craving a chili dog. I try not to be a judgmental person. I do have to admit that I judge gas station chili dog guy a little bit. Those things look violently disgusting. I can't imagine how long they have been sitting there, what they were made from, or what eating that will do to me fifteen minutes after I consume it. Too graphic? Good.

You are absolutely CRAVING this gas station chili dog. You've been thinking about it all day. The time has officially come. It's your lunch break. You walk into the gas station, and there, in all its "glory," you see the chili dog station. I see you there, approach you with an offer and say, "Hey, I've got a deal for you. You can have that chili dog. I'll even buy it for you if you want. Or you can have $1000 dollars."

I pull out of my pocket ten crisp 100 dollar bills with Benjamin Franklin's mug staring you in the face. You can't have both. You can't use the $1000 to buy the chili dog. You get one. Or you get the other.

Which one are you going to choose? You would choose the $1000, wouldn't you? Put yourself in that situation. You would walk out of the gas station so excited. You would call your spouse. You would start imagining all of the things you would do with that money. You know what else would be the case? You wouldn't be craving that chili dog anymore. You found something that you desired more than the chili dog.

That's the first step towards eating healthier. Figure out what it is that you desire more than the foods that you normally crave. You know what will end up happening? The more you eat healthier foods, the more you will desire healthier foods.

CRAVINGS

OUR BODIES CRAVE THINGS THEY ARE USED TO. YOU KNOW ONE THING I HAVE NEVER CRAVED in my entire life? Heroin. I've never craved heroin one time in my life. Do you know why? Because I have never tried heroin. Our bodies crave what we consistently give them. If a person is addicted to a drug for several years and then tries to get off that drug, what happens? They detox. Their body starts craving what it was used to getting, regardless of whether or not that thing was good for it.

Food is the same. Can we be honest? We are addicted to sugar. I've read studies that compare sugar to a drug. I'm not smart enough to know whether or not sugar should be compared to a drug. There are a few things I do know about sugar. We all like it. It's not good for us at all.

Most doctors say the recommended daily dose of sugar is about twenty-five grams per day for women and thirty-eight grams per day for men. They also recommend that kids eat about twelve to fifteen grams of sugar per day. That is what is recommended. So how many grams of sugar are we actually consuming?

The average American is consuming about eighty-five grams of sugar every single day. That equates to about sixty-five pounds of excess sugar consumed every year. That is absolutely astounding. Ladies and gentlemen, we can "sugar" coat this all we want to, be facts are facts. We are addicted to sugar.

The same withdrawal happens when we try to eliminate sugar from our diet that happen when a person tries to stop smoking or get off drugs. You know why you get tired every day at 3 o'clock? Because you are consuming way too much sugar, and your blood sugar is spiking all over the place.

Sugar is bad enough. **James DiNicolantonio** is a cardiovascular research scientist at St. Luke›s Mid-America Heart Institute in Kansas City, Missouri. He recently talked about the effects of sugar as they relate to heart disease.

He also talked about the effects of high fructose corn syrup, which is a sugar substitute. As bad as sugar is, high fructose corn syrup is worse. This is what he said:

"The government subsidizes corn, so high fructose corn syrup is cheaper than sugar, and that's why it's so ubiquitous in our diets," DiNicolantonio explained. "They need to start subsidizing healthy foods. We shouldn't be able to eat a Snickers bar for cheaper than we can eat an apple."

I'm not here to preach to you. I understand there are things related to our health that are completely outside of our control. I do, however, believe that there are many issues we face today health-wise in our country that are caused by a poor diet.

In the 1960's, three percent of children were considered to be in the obese category. Today, almost 20% of children ages two to nineteen are considered obese. In the United States, 29.1 million people are living with diagnosed or undiagnosed diabetes, and about 208,000 people younger than twenty years old are living with diagnosed diabetes. This is according to the National Institute of Health.

Is this just an anomaly? Is this just what happens? Why have we seen that much of a change in less than sixty years? I think it's safe to say the cause is what we are eating. The average American spends $100 per month eating fast food. Almost twenty percent of all meals are eaten in a car. I get it. We are busy. Busy leads to terrible eating habits. We may think it's just temporary. Our eating habits are, quite literally, killing us.

If there is one thing I hear over and over from people it's this. "Eating healthy is just so expensive." A few thoughts about this. First of all eating healthy doesn't always have to be expensive. Most people spend between 15-20 dollars per day on themselves for food. That includes

74

coffee and gas station snacks and vending machines and groceries and everything you consume.

Want to do a fun exercise? God back over the last 30 days and add up every single dollar that you have spent on yourself for food. I realize this may be complicated and that you don't just buy food for yourself if you have a family. How much do you spend on you?

What if eating healthier did cost you more than you are currently spending on yourself? What if the decision to be healthier cost you 50 or 100 dollars a month more than you are currently spending. I don't think it has to. But let's say it does. Are you worth that? I truly believe that what we eat is a window into what we value. What we think about ourselves. If your boss or someone important to you came to your house for dinner would you serve fast food? I doubt it. Why? Because they are important to you. Are you important to you? You should be. You are the most valuable resource you have. It's time to start putting the right fuel into your body to help you run at peak performance. It's time we all start eating like we care deeply about ourselves. If eating better is going to cost more, and in most cases it honestly won't, don't think if it as an expense. Think of it as an investment and you, my friend, are worth investing in.

COMFORT FOOD

FOOD IS ALMOST ALWAYS THE ANSWER TO EVERYTHING. WHEN WE CELEBRATE, WE EAT. WHEN we mourn, we eat. When we are stressed, we eat. Usually things with chocolate. Why do we call the foods we enjoy comfort foods? Because they make us feel better. Do they really? They may make us feel better for a moment. I really don't think we like food as much as we think we do. We just like eating. This is why people eat way past when they are full. Their stomach isn't craving more. It's their taste buds that are controlling the show.

You know what I've learned about myself? Have you ever noticed that when you are trying to eat healthy, it's always the weekends that seem to give you the most trouble? We do fine during the week when every-thing is scheduled and regimented. You know what this tells me? Most of the time, I'm not really hungry; I'm just bored. When we are bored, we eat. A lot.

I don't say this as a person who has arrived. I had atrocious eating habits for thirty-five years, and I am not a perfect eater now. I think we should be able to enjoy the food that we eat. I want to ask you a very important question. How can you get better with your eating habits? Again, this book isn't called chasing perfect; it's called chasing better. Do you eat fast food every day? Could you cut that in half? Do you eat twenty percent of your meals in the car? Could you do ten percent?

BUSY, BUSY, BUSY

LET'S BE HONEST. CAN YOU REALLY EAT A SALAD IN THE CAR WHEN YOU ARE DRIVING AND IN a hurry? You can eat a burger and fries in a hurry. You can't eat a chicken breast with squash with a knife and fork while you drive and navigate lunch hour traffic running fifteen minutes late for a meeting.

A lot of our eating habits are controlled by our schedules. We are just busy. We should be generous people. We should put others before ourselves. However, if there is one area of your life in which you absolutely should be selfish, it's your health.

Moms notoriously put themselves last. Moms are the last ones to eat. The last ones to sit down. The last ones to do everything. I get it. It's the mom in you. It's time for you to be a little selfish. It's time for you to do something for you. How much better of a mom would you be if you were healthy? How much more energy could you have? How much more would your kids enjoy you if you weren't overwhelmed and stressed all the time?

Dads, you aren't off the hook. Can you relate to my story? Running around like crazy only to come home exhausted and tired. Your kids or grandkids just want to enjoy some time with you, but all you want to do is sit down and unwind. You think you are exhausted because of the stress of your job. That may be part of it. Want some honesty? It's your diet.

That's not an easy thing to hear. Trust me, I know. As a person who helps people get healthy every day, I know what it's like to get pushback.

It's amazing how many unhealthy health experts there are in our society. We aren't healthy. But we have an opinion about what you should or shouldn't do in order to be healthy.

STRONGHOLDS

THERE IS A VERY CHRISTIAN WORD CALLED STRONGHOLD. STRONGHOLD IN AND OF ITSELF isn't a Christian word. A stronghold is simply a place that you run to that is fortified to fend off an attack. In the Christian world, a stronghold is something that is difficult to overcome. Something that can be seen as an attack against you.

In the church world, food is a stronghold. I truly believe that food in the church is the acceptable addiction. We talk about drug addiction. We talk about alcoholism. We talk about sex-related addictions. We don't talk about food-related addictions. That's because most pastors are food addicts themselves. Sorry, but it's true.

If the church is going to get healthy physically, the pastors need to own their role. Seventy to seventy-five percent of American pastors today are considered overweight. Again, I understand that some of them may have health issues that cause the weight gain. I'm not discounting that. Let's say that's five percent. That still leaves seventy percent who absolutely are in control of their health.

Ever been to a ministers' breakfast? Look at what we eat. Ever been to a church potluck? Look at what is being served. I understand this isn't popular. This is why I never get surprised when I get pushback about what I do. I expect it and welcome it. I know that I'm dealing with a stronghold. If you are a Christian, if you are a pastor, can I challenge you to take a look at your health and ask yourself what you can do in order to be better? You will never change your health until you realize this is something that needs to change. We don't change things that we don't think are broken.

Paul himself talked about this in First Corinthians 6:19-20 (NIV):

"Do you not know that your bodies are temples of the Holy Spirit, who is in you, whom you have received from God? You are not your own; you were bought at a price. Therefore honor God with your bodies."

Some of us care way more about what our church sanctuary looks like than we care about the food we put into our bodies. I've been to churches that freak out if you bring coffee into the sanctuary because, heaven forbid, coffee spills on the carpet. The reasoning? "This is the House of the Lord. We need to take care of it."

I thought you were the house of the Lord? I thought you were where He resides? Would you be ok with me bringing in a burger and fries into your sanctuary without a napkin? Getting ketchup everywhere and wiping my greasy hands all over the chairs? Why is it ok for you to do that to your body but not ok for someone to do it in a building?

Mad at me yet? Good. This obviously affects way more than people who go to church. This is a societal issue. Our medicine is getting better, and our food is getting worse. We have more access to unhealthy food, and we are less active than we have ever been. That doesn't add up to good things in the long run. You may have been able to get away with eating an entire pizza at midnight when you were twenty and in college. You aren't twenty any more. The problem is, we can't see the effects immediately from a bad diet. We may feel indigestion and lack of energy. We have all bought into the myth that one day we will start eating healthily. Soon we realize that one day never comes.

Are you going to make the decision to change, or are you going to wait until your deteriorating health makes that decision for you? One thing I can promise you, a bad diet WILL catch up to you if you don't change it. So change it.

I've talked to so many people that want to eat better, they just literally don't know what better is. This is precisely why I made the decision to work with a coach to help me. Could I have done it on my own? Possibly. I don't know if I could have done it on my own or not. I just know that I did it when I asked someone to help me. You've heard the definition of insanity, right? Doing the same thing over and over again and expecting different results.

THE POWER OF COMMUNITY

I'VE NEVER REALLY BEEN A GYM RAT. THE GYM HAD ALWAYS SCARED ME UP UNTIL A FEW years ago. We tend to be scared by things we don't understand or feel we are good at. After I lost thirty pounds by changing what I ate, I decided to join a CrossFit box. Talk about sticking out like a sore thumb. I'll never forget my first workout. It was a partner WOD (Workout of the Day) with a girl named Ally. She was about 130 pounds of solid muscle. And she absolutely CRUSHED me during the workout.

I've been going to CrossFit for almost two years, and while I have DEFINITELY seen major progress, I still feel like I'm the worst one in the gym sometimes. I have so much to learn. Everyone in there seems younger, fitter, and better than me. I may not be the strongest one there. I may not put in the best times. One thing I can guarantee is that I will keep showing up. I know that if I keep showing up, eventually I will get the results I desire. I'm so grateful for people who have inspired me on my fitness journey. Matt and Taylor at CrossFit 859. Sarina, Ray, and Dusty at CrossFit 239. All of these people can crush me. They can all out lift me. I have watched them every day for the last two years, and they make me want to be better. Do you want to get stronger and into better shape? Work out with people who can crush you.

Out of all of the chapters in this book, this is the area where you can begin to chase better immediately. You are one meal away from changing your life. Have you ever made a resolution in January to be healthy and failed before the month was over? Me, too. How are you going to make this time different? This may be a battle every day, but I can promise you it is a battle worth fighting. It's a battle that will be impossible for you to win if you are fighting it by yourself.

Community is one of the most important aspects of your health journey. This is why people flock to CrossFit. CrossFit is one of the most amazing communities I have ever been a part of. I have never once felt judged in CrossFit because of what I couldn't do. CrossFit is all about competing with yourself and chasing better every single day.

Get around people who will hold you accountable on what you are eating. People aren't interested in joining a diet. We want to be a part of a community. I love that we are now a part of a health community that has literally impacted millions of lives across the country and soon to be the world. Get around people who inspire you to eat better and be more active. Figure out what it is that you want most and chase it. I don't care how amazing that piece of cheesecake is that you are craving. I can promise you that nothing on planet earth tastes as good as healthy feels.

CHAPTER 7

ALL THE WAY THERE

"To be in your children's memories tomorrow, you have to be in their lives today."

—Barbara Johnson

DISTRACTED SOCIETY

GROWING UP, I SPENT A LOT OF TIME IN CHURCH. I HAD SOME GOOD EXPERIENCES AND SOME not-so-good experiences. I made some amazing, life-long friends, and I met some people who weren't so great. Overall, I am grateful that I grew up the way that I did. I was able to learn some life lessons from some amazing leaders that have stuck with me to this day.

One of my youth pastors growing up was a lady by the name of Jeanne Mayo. Jeanne is one of the most well-known youth pastors ever, and I am blessed to be able to have learned so much from her. Jeanne was, and is to this day, affectionately referred to as "mom" by thousands of people. Not only was Jeanne a phenomenal speaker; she was one of the best listeners I have ever met in my whole life. Jeanne had this gift of making you feel like you were the most important person in the world whenever you had the opportunity to speak with her. She would look you right in the eyes and be so affirming. I cannot begin to describe how good it feels to know that someone has truly heard you.

Listening literally takes zero skill. This is definitely an area that I need to chase better. Can I be honest with you? I REALLY like to talk. You know that guy who sometimes finishes your sentences for you before you even get the chance to? Isn't that guy annoying? I'm that guy. I don't want to be that guy. I just know that, sometimes, I am that guy.

Have you ever noticed that, more often than not, when you are in a discussion with your spouse, you aren't really listening to what they are saying? You are just waiting for them to stop talking so that you can start talking?

Have you ever been a fly on the wall during Facebook debates? Aren't they great? Do people really and truly listen to what someone else is saying when in those kinds of discussions?

"You're wrong. Let me list all of the reasons why." I'm not saying debate is always wrong. I'm not saying it's wrong to want to be right. I just know that I want to be a person who makes other people want to feel heard. I've learned from my wife that, more often than not, she doesn't want me to fix her. She just wants me to understand.

I remember when this began to click for me. We were blessed to be able to have my wife stay at home with our kids when they were too young to be school aged. I remember coming home from work exhausted, as I mentioned before. I was tired. The problem was, so was Julie. I was dealing with people's problems at church all day. She was talking to toddlers all day. When I came home, she just wanted a break, and rightfully so.

I, on the other hand, simply wanted to not speak. I was tired of listening to problems all day. I didn't want to fix anything else. I just wanted to sit and be. I just wanted to literally think about nothing. The big problem was, I wasn't giving the best part of my day to the people who mattered most to me.

I realized that my wife wanted two things from me. She wanted help. She wanted conversation with someone who was older than four years old. She didn't want me to fix anything. I had a hard time getting out of fixing people mode. I probably shouldn't have been in that mode when I was at church either. I guess it's just how I thought people valued me. You are talking to me because you have a problem. I am a guy who fixes problems.

Sometimes, people do want help fixing their problems. Most of the time, people just want to be heard. I've learned that, more often than not, asking people questions helps them solve problems way more than just simply telling them what to do anyway. The only way you can ask someone good questions is if you listen to what they are saying instead of just simply waiting for them to stop speaking.

Of all of the chapters in this book, this one by far is the one that needs the most growth from me. I am not an expert listener; I am not Doctor Phil. I am not a counselor. I was the worst counselor on Planet Earth. I am right there with you. The only difference between me and many other people is I recognize this to be an area of growth for me.

Many people are blind to it. They are blind to how much they speak and how little they listen. They are blind to what other people really and truly need because they think they have the answer instead of just being someone who cares enough to listen.

Listening takes time. Listening take empathy. If there is one thing America lacks GREATLY, it is empathy, which is the ability to see something from somebody else's perspective instead of our own. We lack empathy at work. We lack empathy on social media. We lack empathy when we drive our cars. We definitely lack empathy with the people who live in our own homes.

COMMUNICATING WITHOUT WORDS

BEING THE ONLY MALE IN A HOUSE WITH ALL FEMALES, I RECOGNIZE THAT MORE OFTEN THAN not, girls tend to speak more words in a day than males do. When you ask a young girl to tell you about her day at school, you get a ton of detail.

You hear about every subject, what she had for lunch, who farted in class, and what game they invented during recess.

When you ask a little boy to tell you about his day, he usually responds with, "It was fine. I'm hungry. Can I play video games?"

When I came home each day, I had three girls who wanted to tell me all about their days. When asked about my day, I usually simply responded with, "It was fine."

Girls typically are big fans of details. Guys are big fans of getting to the point. Neither is right. Neither is wrong. It's what makes relationships so fantastically complicated.

If there are two words that describe so many people in our culture today, they would be "busy" and "distracted." We are busier than we have ever been before. We are busy. We are overwhelmed. We are working multiple jobs just to make ends meet. We have money issues. It is absolutely impossible for those things not to impact relationships.

We all know what it means to take work home with us. I'm not sure taking work home with you is completely bad. As someone who works from home, it's impossible not to take work home with me.

WHAT'S NEXT?

THERE ARE SO MANY THINGS, MOST OF WHICH ARE ABSOLUTELY NECESSARY, THAT OCCUPY our time. The bills need to be paid. Kids need to get to gymnastics. Homework needs to be done. The dog needs to go outside to pee. I worry that so much of our time is spent preparing for the next thing that we rarely stop to fully embrace and enjoy the current thing.

Think about your life. Aren't you always looking forward to the next season. Elementary kids can't wait to get into junior high. Junior highers can't wait for high school. High schoolers can't wait for the freedom of college. College students can't wait to get a job and start making money. Those fresh into the work force can't wait to get a better job and start making more money. Those who are in the work force can't wait for retirement. Those in retirement wish they could go back in time and do it all over again.

LISTENING WITH YOUR HEART

ALMOST NOBODY IS HAPPY WITH THE CURRENT STATE THEY ARE IN. WE ARE EITHER LOOKING forward to what is next and hopefully better or looking behind toward a season of life that made us happier than the one we are currently in. I'm not anti-looking forward to the future. I'm not anti-looking backward to reminisce. I am saying we as people traditionally aren't great at fully enjoying and embracing the season we are in. The current messy, stressful, wouldn't-trade-it-for-the-world season.

The busier we are, the more distracted we become. I'm not anti-cell phone. I literally work from my phone. I love technology. I love social media. I pay for Netflix. None of these things are bad.

I've been guilty all too many times of being so engrossed in what I was looking at on my device that I failed to focus on connecting with the actual people I was sharing space with at that given moment. One of the best pieces of advice I've ever been given is, "Wherever you are, be all the way there."

I don't do that very well. This isn't because of my gender, although we as guys tend to lag behind our female counterparts when it comes to focus. Have you ever been in a conversation with someone who was talking to you while scrolling through Instagram? I've been that person. I've been the guy who has been lost in my phone while those most important to me were attempting to connect. I already told you in the previous chapter about my daughter drawing a picture of a chubby dude on a couch scrolling on a phone. That was me.

I don't write this to cast stones in judgment. I'm with you. This is a struggle for me. I live in a distracted world, and, all too often, I have participated. I now realize that if I am in a conversation with someone and I am looking consistently at my phone while they speak, what I am telling them is that what I am looking at on my phone is more important than they are.

Of course, there is a difference between a glance and getting lost into something. I truly desire to be a person who makes others communicating with me feel as if they are truly being heard instead of just simply being noticed. People don't want to just be noticed or acknowledged. They want to be heard. They want to be validated. My goodness do I need a lot of work in this area.

I have a friend who works in the medical field in Ohio. A few days ago, he was sharing an experience he had with a patient in a group of which we are both part. This patient was bragging on him to one of his nurses in the office. This is what she had to say about my friend Rich:

"I sure love Dr. Rich. He listens, not just with his ears, but with his heart."

Is that not the most amazing compliment you have ever heard? I want to be a person who doesn't just listen to what others are saying with my ears. I want to listen with my heart. When you listen with your heart, the person you are communicating with will truly feel not just heard, but understood.

BLACK AND WHITE IN A WORLD OF GRAY

WE TEND TO BE BLACK AND WHITE PEOPLE IN A WORLD THAT IS FILLED WITH GRAY. THIS makes being better at anything extremely difficult. In a world overwhelmed with technology, it's nearly impossible to imagine life without it, which causes us to consistently justify. We start pointing to all of the good things about social media, and there are plenty of them. We start pointing to all of the benefits of text messaging, and there are plenty of them. Most people point to extremes whenever they are trying to defend something about themselves.

We do this in politics. We do this in relationships. "Corey, stop with the 'cellphones are bad' argument. They are necessary. They make life so much better. I don't want to go back to living in 1973."

Me neither. I'm glad I am alive right now, and I love so much about technology. I LOVE my iphone. It's WAY better than your Android. I just sometimes wonder if our lives are run by a device instead of the device being a tool that simply helps make life more convenient.

Have you ever tried to put your phone on the charger when you got home and refused to look at it until the next morning? You begin to spend time with your family, and all of a sudden you look at the clock to see how long it's been since you had your phone, and it's been thirty minutes. You begin to silently panic, wondering about all that you might have missed. The updates that will now forever be buried in your newsfeed, never to be seen by you again because you missed them.

FOMO

LITTLE KIDS DEAL OFTEN WITH THE FEAR OF "NOT WANTING TO MISS OUT." THAT'S WHY THEY don't want to go to bed earlier than you, especially when there is company over. They feel like there is going to be something that will happen, and they will miss out. We pass it off as kids being kids. Are we any different? We refuse to unplug from social media because we are afraid that someone will post something, and we will miss it.

Have you ever gotten a message from a friend asking if you saw their latest social media post? You ask them when they posted, and they say, "ten minutes ago." You know what the sad reality is? Most of the time, we have already seen it. We have seen it because, more often than not, our lives are being lived through a device. It's slowly killing our relationships, and it's slowly killing us in the process.

Who Is paying the price for our constant need to always know what's happening with everyone else? Social media truly is one of the best innovations of all time. It's genius. I use it every day and will continue to use it every day. Just like anything else, of course, it can be abused. Food can be abused. Alcohol can be abused. The Internet can be abused. News channels can be abused. Social media can be abused. Coffee can be abused.

Admittedly, I'm not a coffee drinker. I'm not anti-coffee. I think it's fair to say that we as people love our coffee more than ever. The average American spends about $15 per week on coffee. That's not an astronomical amount. Most people drink coffee because they enjoy it, which is well and good. Others drink coffee simply because they need it. Why do we need it? Because we are exhausted. We are working longer and sleeping less than we ever have. The sleep foundation says that adults over the age of twenty-five should be getting at least seven to nine hours of sleep every night. Most people get between five and six.

Why are we not getting enough sleep? We can look at our busy schedules as a culprit. My opinion is that the biggest culprit contributing to our sleeping less is our smartphones. We put our smartphones next to our beds and find ourselves scrolling away on Instagram or Facebook or Twitter. Pretty soon, we've been scrolling for an hour and are no more tired than we were when we laid our head on the pillow. What's even worse is when we can barely keep our eyes open, and we still scroll. It's like we view sleep as the enemy, and again, like a kid with company over, we are afraid during our time of sleep that we will miss something.

It's hard to argue with the fact that we value sleep less than we value being informed or being entertained. What happens when we get less sleep? We are less productive the next day. We are exhausted when we get home. We don't have much to give to our families.

Can we stop with the "I need my cell phone next to my bed for the alarm" excuse? If that truly is the case, plug your phone in across the room so that when it goes off you physically have to get out of bed every morning to walk over and turn it off.

I'm not anti-putting the phone plugged in next to your bed. I'm anti-excuses. The VAST majority of us don't plug in the phone next to our beds because of the alarm on our phone. We do it so that we can scroll before we go to bed and right when we wake up. What is your lack of sleep costing you? What if getting better at being present with your family was as simple as turning off your phone at night or plugging it in across the room? What if we aren't giving ourselves the best chance to succeed because we are giving the best parts of us to a device instead of to another person?

ONLY GUY IN A HOUSE FULL OF GIRLS

CAN I BE HONEST ENOUGH TO ADMIT THAT, SOMETIMES, IT'S A CHALLENGE FOR ME TO BE THE only guy living in a house filled with girls? I'm not crafty. I'm not someone who necessarily enjoys sidewalk chalk. I don't understand the Barbie world. *High School Musical* isn't something that I would choose to watch if I had an hour to kill. As much as I love Disney World, I can think of a few better ways to spend $5,000 dollars. I don't "do hair." I am learning that what my girls want from me more than anything else is my time. They want me to be available. This is much easier now that I work from home. I am blessed to be able to take them to school every day and be there at the house when they get home. We get to travel in the summer and do all kinds of fun things that we simply weren't able to when they were younger.

We all desire to be free. We want to be free financially and free with our time. Isn't that the American dream? Isn't that what all of us are chasing? Freedom is the ability to do what you want, when you want. Many people have the financial ability to do what they want, but they don't have the time. Others have all the time in the world, but they don't have the resources to do what they want to do. We want both. We want to have the time and resources necessary to live the life we choose to live and live it well.

True freedom is the ability to spend quality and consistent time with the ones who matter most to us. Isn't that why we work so hard? We don't want to get to the end of our lives and have nobody to share the fruits of our labor with. We want a best friend we can grow old with. We want kids to pour into and grandkids to spoil. We just need to remember not to focus so much on what life will look like thirty years from now that we fail to take advantage of the moment we have today.

What we say isn't what we believe. What we do is what we believe. Our words don't define us nearly as much as our actions do. A person can say they are a Christ follower. That's fine. Do your actions back that up?

If I were to ask you who the most important people to you in the world are, what would you say? You would say your family, right? Your wife, your husband, your kids, your siblings, your best friends. Our check-books tell us what we value the most. Whatever it is we spend our money on is a good indicator of what we value.

Another good indicator is how you spend your time. Who do you give the best parts of your day to? Do you give your best parts of your day to your job? Video games? Fantasy football? Netflix? The gym? Who gets the best parts of you? I know that we all say that our family means more to us than anyone else. Does our time back that up? I think if most of us were honest with ourselves and the way we spent our time was the true measure of who we cared the most about, what we would discover is that the person we care the most about is ourselves. Ouch.

Yes, I know we all have to work. Yes, I know all of the excuses. Remember, I am way better at justifying than you. The only reason I know this to be true is because of my own experience. Maybe yours is different. I just very much doubt it.

Listen, I'm sure you care a great deal about your family. I'm sure they mean a lot to you. I didn't ask you if they meant a lot to you. I asked you what was most important. Maybe I'm off base. At the very least, I've opened up a very important can of worms. Maybe you can chuck this chapter out the window and move on to the next one. I'm guessing some of us just got a very healthy dose of reality.

HERSHEY'S FOR THE WIN

I SAW A COMMERCIAL ON TV A FEW YEARS AGO THAT ABSOLUTELY GRIPPED ME. I'M NOR-mally not a commercial guy. I change the channel or pause and fast-for-ward like the rest of the civilized world. For some reason, I was watching the commercials on this particular day.

Of all things, it was a Hershey's commercial. The song playing in the background is a version of Steve Winwood's "Higher Love."

In the commercial, there is a little girl who desperately wants her dad's attention. The problem is, her dad is always working. She gets an idea. She empties her piggy bank, goes to a local print shop, and gets a life-sized cardboard cutout of her dad. She takes this cardboard cutout of her dad with her everywhere. When you see the commercial, it's actually a little bit heartbreaking. You get the impression that this little girl is so wanting to spend time with her dad that she creates a cardboard cutout to carry around with her to remind her of her father.

Toward the end of the commercial, you see a picture of her dad looking at his computer on a video conference call. When it pans back, its actually the cardboard cutout version that the real father stood at his desk. The cardboard cutout dad attended the video work conference while the real dad made s'mores with his daughter in the kitchen. Well done, Hershey. Well done. Go to YouTube and search for "Hershey's cardboard cutout" and watch the commercial for yourself. It's gripping.

That commercial forced me to ask myself some very important questions. Who was getting the best parts of my day? Was working getting the best of me? Or was my family getting the best of me? As I sit down to write this, my family is packing for a two-week-long vacation to Disney World in Orlando, Florida. I can't wait to spend some uninterrupted time with my girls at their favorite place on the planet. Not just my daughters' favorite place. It's my wife's favorite, too. Fine! Get off my back. I love it too ok. There, I said it. Are you happy now?

We will go on all of the rides. Stand in line to see all of the princesses. Fight the crowds as we watch a fireworks show and pay an ungodly amount of money for food. We will love every second of it.

I'm learning more and more that my wife doesn't expect a perfect husband. My daughters don't expect a perfect dad. They expect a dad who shows up. My parents worked very hard when I was growing up to provide for four kids. They had to make a lot of sacrifices that I'm sure I will never know about. I'll never forget my dad driving forty-five minutes in the rain to switch cars with me because the car I drove didn't have air conditioning, and he didn't want me to have to drive back home without A/C on a hot summer day.

I'll never forget my mom sneaking notes into my bowling bag telling me how proud she was of me on days that I had tournaments that she was unable to attend because of work. Or my dad making a "Bake-O-Meter" sign that he held up in the stands at my little league baseball games announcing to the world what my batting average was every time I got a hit.

Mom. Dad. Husband. Wife. Showing up doesn't take a lot of talent. It just takes time and energy. I encourage you to ask yourself the question of who matters most to you in this world. Then look at your schedule to see if your time and attention reflect that. You can't do anything about how you spent your time yesterday. If changes need to be made, make them. Don't just tell your family you love them. Show them. Give your best self to the ones who matter the most to you.

CHAPTER 8

ONE THING WE CAN ALL CHASE BETTER

"The great gift of human beings is that we have the power of empathy."

—Meryl Streep

AFFIRMATION ADDICTION

I WAS BLESSED TO GROW UP IN A HOUSE WHERE I WAS THE OLDEST OF FOUR BOYS. Competition and sibling rivalry were things that seemed to come naturally. It really didn't matter what it was, we would find a reason to compete. Who can get dressed first? Who can finish their food first to ensure they get the seconds?

From the very moment we are born, we are in competition. Our parents compare us to other babies. We want to know what percentile our kids are. How big is their head? How tall are they? How much do they weigh? Those are all good things to know. What we really want to know is, how does my kid compare to your kid? Whenever you are in a conversation with someone else who also has children, it usually revolves around each one telling stories about what exploits their offspring accomplished in the previous week. We do this because we are proud of our kids. We also do it because we like comparison.

There aren't too many things we take more personally than our children. Rightfully so. We are their protectors. We love them more than we love ourselves. We would gladly trade our lives for theirs. I've also learned that being a parent is challenging because it forces me to work on areas of my life that I don't always want to work on. I don't enjoy being selfless. I don't enjoy giving up the TV. I don't always enjoy listening to others tell me about how great their kids are. Can I say that? I'm sure other people don't enjoy hearing the same from me either.

Just like little kids with siblings, we as people always have this instinct to fight for, protect, and defend ourselves even if the threat we are facing exists solely in our own imagination. Protecting ourselves is an instinct we are all born with. You don't have to teach a child to run away from something chasing them. We know how to do that. You could argue the first thing programmed into us when we are being made is, "Protect yourself at all costs."

This isn't all bad. We should protect ourselves. We should fight for what we want. We should be proud of our kids. We should love ourselves. We should even like ourselves. As with just about everything else in this life, there is balance. Where am I going with this?

It's been said that if you are ever in a situation where you are conversing with someone and you don't know what to talk about, ask them about themselves. Everyone enjoys talking about themselves. Why is that? Because EVERY person has a desire to be affirmed. As kids, we want to be affirmed by our parents. As teenagers, we want to be affirmed by our friends. As adults, we want to be affirmed by our peers. As parents, we want to be affirmed by our kids. We are starving for affirmation.

We long for words of affirmation from people almost as much as we long for food to eat and air to breathe. Anyone who tells you they don't care what anyone thinks of them is lying. Of course we care what people think of us. Should this control our life? Of course not. But we are naïve if we say that what other people think about us doesn't have an impact on who we are or who we become.

If protecting ourselves is an instinct we are born with, if looking out for ourselves above all else is a characteristic of all people, why should we even bother getting better at something like this? How can I "get better," at looking out for myself? Is that something I even need to do?

This is such an interesting question, and, like so many things in life, I'm not sure there is a black and white answer. We long for things to be black and white. We want to know what is right and what is wrong. While black and white exist, while right and wrong exist, we live in a world that is filled with gray. And it's beautiful.

Do I care about others, or do I care about myself? Yes.
Do I put my own dreams first, or do I put other people ahead of myself? Yes.

Confused yet? Me, too. Isn't it great? Isn't life so amazingly complicated? I'm glad life isn't easy. I'm glad I don't always have the answer to everything.

THE POWER OF EMPATHY

THERE IS A WORD IN OUR LANGUAGE THAT JUST MAY BE ONE OF MY FAVORITE WORDS. IT'S a word that every person reading this book, every person who calls themselves an American, every person who calls themselves a human, could get better at doing. The lack of us putting into practice this one word is the reason why we as Americans are more divided than we have ever been. We can blame politicians if we want to, but that would be too easy. We can blame a political party. We can blame a religion. We can blame our parents, or the school system, or lament the fact that we no longer live in "the good old days."

Do you want to know why we are so divided in our country? We are divided because we don't do empathy very well. What exactly is empathy? Empathy is defined as, "the ability to understand and share the feelings of another."

Think about this. Do you know any four-year-olds who are very good at empathy? Yes, I know. Your four-year-old is amazing. I'm talking about all of the other four-year-olds. Do you know any four-year-olds, besides yours, who are really good at showing empathy? The answer to that question is a big, resounding no. I'm just going to guess that yours isn't great at it either. I know you are super parent, but your kid is four. Do you know what four-year-olds care about at four? Themselves. I'm not calling them spoiled. I'm calling them four. You can unclench now. ☺

Most of the time when people get into "discussions" with someone else, whether in person or on social media, we aren't really listening to what the other person is saying. We are simply waiting for them to stop talking so that we can share our opinion. We aren't listening to understand; we are listening in order to share a response.

I think America has developed an addiction to being right. We simply want to win the argument. I have often asked myself this as I browse social media observing debate after debate. What are we really wanting to accomplish? What is the win? Are you thinking that the other person, in response to our spectacularly well-written response, is going to say, "You know something, you are right. I was wrong. Let's be friends."

Is that what we want them to say? Are we trying to be right, or do we really just think it's our responsibility to share our opinion about everything? I'm not saying discussion is bad. Debate can be important. Debate can even sometimes be necessary. Do we REALLY need to debate EVERYTHING, though? Can't there just be sometimes that we read something and don't feel the constant desire to share our opinion about everything that is said or written? Just a thought.

MEAN TWEETS

SOCIAL MEDIA IS MAKING EMPATHY MORE AND MORE CHALLENGING. IT IS MUCH EASIER TO be a jerk on social media than it is when the other person is looking at you in the face. One of my favorite segments to watch on TV is the mean tweets by Jimmy Kimmel. Basically, Jimmy has celebrities who come on his show read mean things that people tweet at them on Twitter. People are mean!

My favorite part of this segment is the responses of the celebrities who read the tweets. Most of them take it in stride and laugh it off. I can almost guarantee that every person in the spotlight has been on the receiving end of hate mail. Social media has just made hate mail a whole lot easier.

People look at celebrities and think, "They make millions of dollars; they should be able to take it." That just might be the dumbest argument I've ever heard. Does someone making a million dollars a year all of a sudden have no feelings? They have money. Good for them. They are also a human person who probably values many of the same things that I do.

One of my good friends, Dr. Wayne Anderson, has told me on numerous occasions, "Beliefs divide people, and values unite them."

He is so right. Having beliefs is great. We all believe in something. The problem is, not everyone believes the same things that we do. What do we do when someone else believes something that is completely opposite of what we believe? Are we able to separate who that person is from what they believe?

If you are a church person, I'm going to say something that you may not like. Stick with me. I'm not saying you shouldn't try to grow your church. I'm not telling you that you shouldn't tell your story of what faith has done for you. By all means, proselytize. You should. If it's something you care about, you should tell other people about it.

It's just important for you to realize what you are up against. It's not wrong to share your beliefs. It is divisive, though. Don't be surprised when sharing your beliefs makes some people upset. Don't stop doing it. Just understand not everyone is going to like it. You really have two choices. You can develop a "Who cares about what they think?" attitude, which can be useful. Or maybe we can stop wondering what people believe in and start asking ourselves why they believe it.

LEARNING THE STORY OF OTHERS

EVERYONE HAS A STORY. EVERYONE BELIEVES WHAT THEY BELIEVE FOR A REASON. THAT REAson usually has a lot to do with something that has happened to them or something they have experienced. Our belief systems come primarily from our experiences.

What if we stopped trying to convert people and started trying to understand them? I get it. If you are a person of faith, you have a genuine concern for the person you are in conversation with. Ready for a challenging question? You're not going to like it. Are you trying to convert someone to a faith, or are you just trying to get someone to think like you think?

Are we trying to covertly baptize people into the religion of us? Where people think like us, like the same music as us, and have the same style as us? Are you mad at me yet? I can live with that.

What if we all became passionate about understanding? I fully realize this is messy. I fully realize I don't have all of the answers. What if our mission, as the amazing author Bob Goff says, was really as simple as "Love Everybody, Always."

"But what if they..."

Everybody. Always. Isn't that what Jesus did? Isn't the goal of Christianity to be like Jesus? Isn't that the point of the whole deal? Did Jesus love everybody, always? Didn't He pray that God would forgive the very people nailing him to a cross?

How are you doing at loving everybody, always? I highly suggest picking up Bob Goff's book if you want to be challenged in this area.

This is obviously way bigger than church. For those of you who aren't church people, that is completely ok. Much of my life was formed inside of a church, so its very difficult for me to write about this subject without filtering it through those lenses.

This isn't just a church issue. It's a people issue. Can I let you in on a little secret? We aren't the first generation to fight about religion and politics. People have been fighting about religion and politics since there was such a thing as religion and politics. If that really is the case, is there any hope? Are religion and politics something that people will always fight about? Yes.

This is not a plea to rid the world of disagreement. There is no perfect utopia where we all dance and sing folk songs together while sipping on herbal tea and laughing hysterically arm in arm with our once sworn enemy. Maybe that exists in another life. It doesn't in this one.

Of course we won't be best friends with everyone. Of course there will just be some people who drive us crazy. Of course we won't invite certain people to go on a family vacation with us. People will always gravitate towards some people and away from some others.

You don't have to be best friends with someone in order to do your best to understand them. I've learned that when I learn why a person is the way that they are, it usually helps me have a lot more grace toward them.

FLIPPING THE SCRIPT

I WAS RECENTLY AT A MEMORIAL SERVICE. WE WERE CELEBRATING THE LIFE OF AN AMAZING woman named Lori Anderson. She passed away much too soon but lived an extraordinary life impacting a massive number of people. At her funeral, someone was sharing about her life and began to talk about how she handled situations when someone would start talking negatively to her about someone else.

Every time someone would speak negatively to Lori about someone else, she would counteract that negative comment with something positive. She would search for anything she possibly could. I love that so much. How many of us honestly do that? When someone comes to you spewing negativity about someone, especially if its someone you know, how do you respond to that?

Do we allow that person to take us down into the pit of negativity with them? I'm guessing most of us would probably say that more often than we would like, we go down into the pit. Words are powerful. They affect us, whether they are words that we speak or words that we allow ourselves to listen to. Most of us are very easily influenced. We don't know if the words being spoken to us by someone else about another person are true or not. Most people believe the things they choose to believe. If you have a friend who challenges you in your negativity, stick close to that friend.

WHAT TYPE OF FRIEND ARE YOU?

MOST OF US HAVE TWO DIFFERENT TYPES OF FRIENDS. WE HAVE THE FRIEND WE KNOW WE can turn to if we want to complain and talk negatively about someone. We also have that friend who helps us see the best in a situation or a person. Which type of person do you want to be? You are on a list right now. Your friends have placed you in a category. Are you the one they complain about people to? Or are you the one who helps get them back on track when they start to fall below the line?

I think we can all agree that speaking negatively about others probably isn't the best. We know we probably shouldn't do it. Comedian Jim Gaffigan compares gossip to eating McDonald's fries. The more you do it, the more you crave it. Nobody can eat just one McDonald's fry. Jim goes on to talk about how ironic it is that people who look down on those who eat McDonald's have their own McDonald's that just may be served up a little differently.

That's why we talk negatively about others, right? We do so in order to make ourselves feel better about us. We put others down so that in some way, we will be puffed up. It's like the stock market. If you buy a stock, it's because someone else is selling theirs. You can't sell a stock unless someone else is willing to purchase it at the price you are wanting to sell it. There is always a transaction. There is a cause and effect. We tear others down so that we can lift ourselves up. The problem is, this doesn't work. And if it does work, it certainly doesn't last.

THE NEGATIVITY CRASH

TALKING NEGATIVELY ABOUT OTHERS IS KIND OF LIKE LIVING OFF OF ENERGY DRINKS. Energy drinks like Red Bull have a TREMENDOUS amount of sugar meant to give you a short spike in energy. They work. The problem is Newton's Law. What goes up must come down. If you dramatically spike your energy, you are dramatically spiking your blood sugar. And if it dramatically spikes, it will dramatically fall, which means you will either crash or it's time for another energy drink.

What does that have to do with us speaking negatively? We think speaking negatively about others is going to make us feel better, and it might, for a short while. The problem is, a crash is coming. The intent for most people when we speak negatively about others, whether we admit it or not, is to put them down. We put them down, and we push ourselves up. Deep down, we don't want to be this way. I don't think we want to be negative. It's just easier. Negativity is a quicksand that is extremely difficult to get out of.

You won't find too many people who will tell you that living on energy drinks is good for you. They do it out of perceived necessity as opposed to because they think it is actually good for them. If you want to have a lot of energy, it's truly about learning to control your blood sugar so that you eliminate the spikes and crashes that come from excess sugar and caffeine.

The same applies with how we handle negativity. You may get an initial rush when you are in a negative conversation. It may make you feel better for a moment. But a crash is coming. You don't like that you are negative. I don't like it when I am. Ask 100 people what they like best about themselves. You will not get one person to tell you, "I'm really good at talking badly about people."

We don't want to admit that we do this. Nobody is proud of how negative they are. Nobody likes that about themselves. Think of the happiest and most contented people that you know. Are they people who consistently speak negatively about others? How do those people respond when people start to speak negatively around them?

What kind of person do you want to be? You know what I have learned? When I force myself to think something positive about someone who is driving me crazy, my mindset towards them tends to shift. I begin focusing less on what they do that I don't agree with and more on the contributions they bring to society. I truly believe that I can learn something from EVERYONE.

It is important for us to remember that every person has a story. Every person has a reason why they are the way they are. We all have scars.

MY NEW FAVORITE MOVIE

MY NEW FAVORITE MOVIE IS *THE GREATEST SHOWMAN*. I SAW IT FOUR TIMES IN THE THEATER. Admittedly, I didn't know a ton about P.T. Barnum before watching the movie. Turns out, in real life he was kind of a jerk. *The Greatest Showman* is a story about his life with a few creative liberties taken. I don't care about the creative liberties. I don't care how accurate the movie was. I loved the story.

If you haven't seen the movie yet, please stop right now and go watch it. I mean it. Put this book down and go rent or buy this movie. Watch it and then watch it again. Just don't forget to pick this book back up when you are finished. The soundtrack is outstanding. I'm listening to it as I write this.

In the movie, P.T. Barnum is tired of living an average life. He has had his challenges. He marries the woman of his dreams and has two beautiful daughters. After facing financial challenges, he decides to purchase a run-down building and turn it into a museum of sorts.

After not enjoying much success, he decides to turn the museum into a show featuring people who are considered outcasts. He finds Tom Thumb, who was extraordinarily short and was tired of being made fun of. He finds a woman who has a beautiful singing voice but also has a beard. He brings together an army of misfits to put on a show for people to come watch and, in many cases, laugh at.

Many people are uncomfortable with the show. They are uncomfortable with the people who are in the show because they are different. In one of the most defining scenes of the movie, the bearded lady sings a song called, "This is Me." Here are just a few lines from the song.

"I am not a stranger to the dark Hide away, they say 'Cause we don't want your broken parts I've learned to be ashamed of all my scars Run away, they say No one'll love you as you are

But I won't let them break me down to dust I know that there's a place for us For we are glorious

When the sharpest words wanna cut me down I'm gonna send a flood, gonna drown them out I am brave, I am bruised I am who I'm meant to be, this is me Look out 'cause here I come And I'm marching on to the beat I drum I'm not scared to be seen I make no apologies, this is me."

I dare you to watch this scene and not get a little emotional. If you have an ounce of humanity in you, it hurts you to see someone else get made fun of. I wanted to burst through the screen and look at each of the characters in this movie and tell them they had value. They had purpose.

Does any rational adult enjoy seeing kids get picked on by other kids? When we see someone get made fun of, it makes something inside of us rise up. We long to rush to the defense of that person. That's called empathy.

Here's my question: Are you happier when you are judging, or are you happier when you are trusting? When you judge, criticize, or critique others consistently, does that honestly make you feel better? The more we criticize, the more critical we become.

I've never met an overly critical person in my life that I would describe as a happy individual. Isn't that the American dream? We just want to be happy. That's why we work so hard. We want to be happy. Does constantly thinking negatively and speaking negatively about others truly make you happy?

I get it. Most of us have trust issues. We don't like giving others the benefit of the doubt because they may use that benefit to take advantage of us. I would rather give someone the benefit of the doubt and get hurt than trust no one and be miserable.

I challenge all of us to get better at standing up for those who have no one to stand up for them. Find the lost and forgotten. Find the outcasts. Make it your mission each and every day to find someone whom life has beaten up, and, with every ounce of conviction you can muster, look at them in the face and tell them they have value.

What would make you feel better about yourself? Are you happier with you when you are tearing someone down, or are you happier when you are building someone up? Can I challenge you to force yourself to find the good in everyone? I get it. Some people require you to look a little harder than others. You aren't even necessarily looking for the good in them for their sake; you are doing it for yours. Aren't you glad that there are people in this world that look past all your garbage and love you anyway?

You will be happier as a person if you search hard for the good in others. Fight the urge to be critical. Fight the urge to trust nobody. Fight the urge to be just like all of the other voices in our world that are quick to rush to judgement. Believe in others. Give others the benefit of the doubt. Give yourself permission to trust.

CHAPTER 9

ENCOURAGEMENT

"Correction does much, but encouragement does more."

—Johann Wolfgang von Goethe

WHAT ARE YOU LOOKING FOR?

I WAS ONCE AT A LEADERSHIP EVENT WHERE THE SPEAKER WAS TALKING ABOUT NEGATIVITY. There were about 1,000 people in the room at the time. He said, "If there were 998 positive people in this room and two of you were negative, and if we put one negative person at the front and the other all the way in the back, by the end of the day today, you two knuckleheads would find each other."

Isn't that so true? We tend to find exactly what we are looking for. If we want to find someone to complain to, we don't have to look very hard. Negativity is everywhere around us. It fills our timelines. It's on our news stations. It fuels our work conversations. No wonder we are unhappy. Think about the news we watch for a second. Is there ever good news on the news? It's always bad. We continuously feed ourselves endless streams of negativity and wonder why we aren't happy. The reason is that what we continuously feed continuously grows. That's a law of nature.

STARVING FOR ENCOURAGEMENT

WHILE NEGATIVITY IS PREVALENT AND AVAILABLE QUITE LITERALLY AT OUR FINGERTIPS, WE live in a world that is absolutely starving for encouragement. People will do almost anything for someone else to notice and affirm them. We want to stand out. We want to feel useful and appreciated. Most people spend their entire day getting beaten up by life. This is why empathy is so important to me. I understand that every person I meet has a story and that something has probably beaten them up today. Most likely multiple things. Life doesn't need my assistance to constantly pull down the life of someone else. Life is pretty good at trying to pull others down without me. My job isn't to pull people down. My job is to continuously try to lift them back up.

We all learned this from school. Whenever someone picks on someone else, it's really just an attempt to lift themselves up. It truly has nothing to do with the person getting picked on and everything to do with the person dishing it. The person dishing it doesn't care about the person they are making fun of. They only care about lifting themselves up to look better. The problem is the person getting picked on continuously internalizes it to the point where they eventually believe what people keep saying about them. People who continuously get picked on almost never have very high self-esteem. Why? Because more often than not, our self-esteem is high or low based on the words that other people speak to us. If others speak well of us, we tend to think highly of ourselves. If others consistently bash us, we tend to think poorly of ourselves. Of course this isn't ALWAYS the case.

As we grow and mature, we tend to understand that not everyone will like us, and we do our best to surround ourselves with a tribe that does believe in and accept us for who we really are without allowing the negativity to control us anymore.

AMERICA'S PROBLEM

AMERICA HAS A PROBLEM. AMERICA HAS A LOT OF PROBLEMS. SCHOOL SHOOTINGS ARE happening at an unprecedented rate. This isn't a gun control position, though we have to get to a point that we can have unemotional and logical dialogue about this topic, because, obviously, something we are doing isn't working.

If you look at the profiles of those who are committing the vast majority of these school shootings, they are almost exclusively Caucasian males who have a history of getting made fun of because they are different. Getting picked on is not even close to a valid excuse as to why a person would ever choose to inflict harm on another.

We keep having debates about guns and their place in our society, and those are discussions we need to have. Our world is different than it was 300 years ago. We have to come together to figure out how we can change for the better.

You and I may not ever be in the room when this topic is discussed in chambers in Washington, D.C. While we certainly can and should vote whenever legislation on this is presented to the public, there is something everyone can do right now to do our part to help make our country and our schools safer.

Before I tell you what I tell you, again, I want to say I know fully well this won't solve all of the problems. I know this is way more complicated that what I'm about to propose. But what if we all started looking at simple things we can do in order to make our world better and our schools safer? If 99.9 percent of these crimes are committed by someone who is different and consistently made fun of, what if we as parents taught our kids to look for those kids who are constantly getting picked on and befriend them?

I understand this is a big ask. I also understand that most of us do teach our kids to be this way. Just because I teach my kid what they should do doesn't mean they actually will. I understand this is a polarizing topic. More kids are getting shot in schools. More kids are killing themselves. More kids are depressed than ever before. Why is that? Because our world is more negative than it has ever been, and social media has made it easier to publicize that negativity.

People have a strong need for connection. We do not like to be alone. We do not like to feel isolated. We want to be a part. We love being a part of inside jokes. We long to laugh and be accepted. We just want to belong to something.

When people feel isolated and alone, they tend to do irrational things. It's so easy for me to just get focused on me while ignoring people all around me. I get tunnel vision. Have you ever had a really bad toothache? Tooth pain is the worst. Your whole world literally stops, and all you can think about is how bad your tooth hurts.

We get that way sometimes. We get focused on ourselves. We focus on our hurt. We focus on our agendas so much that the cries others make just to be noticed fall on deaf ears. We don't ignore them because we are bad people. We are just distracted people. It's really hard to focus on others when all we do is focus on ourselves. Is it wrong to focus on yourself? Of course not. It's completely normal. I just have to believe that it's possible to focus on both. A switch flips inside of us when we come to the realization that our purpose on this planet is to love and serve others.

Do you want your business to grow? Focus on loving and serving others. Do you want to enlarge your friendship and influence circle? Focus on loving and serving others. Many good things happen when a person transitions from being unconscious to conscious. When we go from being unaware to aware. There are opportunities to love and encourage people everywhere we go, every single day. All we need to do is lift up our eyes.

This all seems so simple and, honestly, a little too easy. Could the answer to the lack of happiness in our world today really be this simple?

PERMISSION TO GOSSIP

HAVE YOU EVER HEARD IT SAID THAT YOU SHOULDN'T TALK BEHIND SOMEONE'S BACK? WE were all taught that at an early age. Do we live by that rule? Most people don't. What if I gave you permission to talk behind other people's backs? I know. You don't need my permission, but go with me. Talking behind someone's back isn't what is wrong. Talking negatively about someone behind their back is what makes it wrong.

If you speak negatively about someone behind their back, odds are they will never know. It's probably not going to affect their life very much. It will greatly affect yours, though.

The funny thing about our words is that oftentimes we say that words we speak about others have a big impact on them. That is true. I truly believe that the words we say about others have an even bigger impact on us. The more negative your words are towards others, the more negative you will be as a person. Each of us are tied to the words we say whether we like it or not. In the Bible, James says that life and death really do lie in the power of the tongue.

What if I told you it is ok to talk behind someone's back as long as those words you are saying are positive? Want to know what's even better than talking about someone positively behind their back? Telling them to their face.

I've learned something about myself. So often, I will be in conversation with someone, and the conversation moves towards the topic of someone else not in the room, I begin to compliment the absent person. Before too long, I begin asking myself a question, "Does the person I am currently saying nice things about even know I think that way about them?"

I have a conviction. A core belief. A rule that I try and live by. Any time I think something positive about someone else, I make sure they know that. Communication has never been easier. We have Facebook and Instagram and text messages and phones that actually allow you to dial a number and use words to speak to another human person.

What if we made encouraging people for no reason at all normal? People get torn down by life every single day. People have money problems and relationship problems and work problems and their favorite sports team losing the night before problems. Don't laugh. It's a problem for some of us.

For many people, life is an absolute grind. It's challenging. Have you ever seen the movie *The Princess Bride*? If not, as soon as you get done watching *The Greatest Showman*, go rent *The Princess Bride*.

It's an older movie that has truly become a cult classic. In the movie, Wesley is desperately trying to save the woman he loves, Buttercup, from the ruthless and evil Humperdink. In his attempt to save Buttercup, Wesley gets captured by the evil forces of Humperdink, and they begin to torture Wesley. They hook Wesley up to a machine that is designed to inflict pain as well as suck years of his life away.

Doesn't life seem that way sometimes? Our jobs are sucking years from our lives. The stress we deal with is sucking years from our lives. Life itself is sucking life away. Life was made to be lived and enjoyed, and yet so many people are just simply trying to survive and make it. Nobody needs my help sucking life away. My job isn't to suck the life away from anyone. My job is to do whatever I can to add years back on.

LESSONS FROM DESMOND DOSS

THE FOUNDATIONS OF PEOPLE'S LIVES TODAY ARE BEING TORN DOWN BY CIRCUMSTANCES every single day. I simply want to take one brick that has fallen at a time and place it back on the wall. I love the movie *Hacksaw Ridge*. In the true story, Desmond Doss is a conscientious objector to World War II. He has made a vow to never touch a firearm, but still wants to serve his country by joining the army as a medic. After facing a lot of opposition from officers and fellow soldiers, Doss joins the army. When asked why he is joining the army, Doss says,

"While everybody else is taking life, I'm going to be saving it. With the world so set on tearing itself apart, it doesn't seem like such a bad thing to me to wanna put a little bit of it back together."

I think it's safe to say that we live in a world today that is occupied with a lot of people intending to tear others down. We may not be in the middle of World War III at the moment. That doesn't mean our world isn't set on tearing itself apart. People have been fighting since people were people. People will fight as long as there is such a thing as people. Pride and ego are things we will never be able to do away with completely. Because of that, so many employ a "why bother" mentality.

Everyone else is content to tear others down in order to prop themselves up. Why shouldn't I join in? You shouldn't join in for two reasons. The first is that person you are tearing down doesn't need your assistance. They feel torn down already. The second is you may think you are putting the other person down, but every negative word you speak about someone else is just pushing you further away from the person you long to be. I truly believe that speaking negatively about others harms you infinitely more than it harms them. Speaking negatively of others keeps you trapped in a pit of blame and shame. You start to focus too much on what other people are doing and not enough on what you can do to improve yourself.

Our world longs for genuine, encouraging friendships. We long for people to breathe life into us. Think about the people you love hanging around. Don't you love being around people who are positive and bring the most out of you? I'm not saying we can't tell others the truth. My friend and mentor, Dan Valentine, always tells me that you will attract more bees with honey than you will with vinegar. He's right. Vinegar is gross. Yes, even on French Fries. There are two types of people in the world: those who put vinegar on their fries and those who are normal and sane. See how easy it is to fall below the line and be negative? I just did it right there. My apologies. Sort of.

DOUBLE DOG DARE

I DARE YOU TODAY TO SEND AN ENCOURAGING TEXT FOR NO REASON TO FIVE PEOPLE. PICK five people. Search through your phone or your Facebook friends list. Write their names down and, one at a time, send them a well-thought-out, genuine encouragement. It doesn't need to be long, but it does need to be genuine. Copy and paste is a great tool, but not when you are trying to genuinely encourage someone. This needs to be personal and unique to them. This takes literally less than sixty seconds, but it can provide such an incredible boost to the person on the receiving end.

Here's what I know. If you spend five minutes of your day encouraging a few people, you will have made a PROFOUND impact on their life. People don't throw away encouraging notes. They keep them. They keep them for a long time. Why do they do this? Because encouraging messages bring life long after they are originally read. Maybe an encouraging message from you is exactly what that person needs to make it through a long, difficult day dealing with difficult people.

I try and send out at least 10 personalized encouraging messages to people every day. I send them to clients, friends, family members, or people I have never even met in person. I want to add life with my words. Want to get encouraging messages from me? Follow me on social media!

INNER JERK

I WENT TO CHEESECAKE FACTORY A FEW DAYS AGO TO EAT LUNCH BY MYSELF. SOME PEOPLE have a complex about eating alone. I truly enjoy it. When I got there, two servers approached my table. One was training the other one. The one who was training announced that she was training. She stumbled through the specials. She got my drink order wrong. She was actually shaking as she brought my food to me and spilled my drink all over me as she placed my food on the table in front of me. I had two choices in that moment. I could have demanded a free meal. I could have been furious that, of all people, I had to be stuck with the person who was training. Do they know who I am? Do they know I'm heading into a very important meeting after this? My goodness, Corey, let it go.

The good news is, I didn't react that way. I'm not saying I've not reacted that way in my head before. Can we be honest? We all have an inner jerk that resides inside of us. That inner jerk demands first-class treatment. That inner jerk gets annoyed when they have to wait. They get annoyed when someone takes their parking spot or orders the last blueberry scone at Starbucks.

Thankfully, my inner jerk didn't come out when the server in training dumped my drink all over me. I told her it was seriously fine. She asked me if she could pay for my meal. I told her that wouldn't be necessary.

She got me another drink. She replaced my meal. I could tell she was visibly shaken. The time came for her to deliver my bill. You could tell she was very apprehensive. I gave her my card. I paid for the meal, which was around $20. I left her a $20 tip and wrote "Great job," on the receipt.

I don't normally look for the server's response after I leave a tip, but I did this time. She took the folio, went to her station and opened it, and started to cry. I don't know what her day was like. I don't know why she has this job. Maybe she is a single mom. Maybe her mom just got diagnosed with cancer. Maybe this is a second job she picked up to pay off debt. I don't know her story. I do know that I'd much rather be the guy who leaves a 100% tip after getting a drink spilled on me than the guy who demands a free meal because someone made a simple mistake. Who do you want to be?

I'm sure you've heard what the Bible teaches about this, right? You reap what you sow. Many times we think this only has to do with money. If you are generous, you will reap generosity. If you are selfish, you will reap selfishness. This principle has to do with so much more than money. Do you long for encouragement? Be honest. Get past the bravado that you don't need other people to say nice things to you. You do. I do. Get over yourself. We shouldn't live for compliments, but it's ignorant to think that we don't need encouragement from others. We all do.

DEFLECTING

NOW THAT WE'VE GOTTEN PAST THE INITIAL PUSHBACK OF, "I DON'T NEED ENCOURAGE-ment," go with me for a second. We all need encouragement. We all feel better when we get it. We've all been the recipient of a well-timed word of encouragement on that day when nothing seems to be going right for us. We shouldn't be fishing for compliments. We all know how to do that, right? We deflect or speak negatively about ourselves in hopes that someone will build up what we have torn down. I used to do this a lot. Most of us don't know how to receive compliments or words of encouragement. We are constantly trying to deflect.

I remember when people used to come up to me and tell me that I had done a good job speaking on a Sunday. I used to say things like, "Oh, it wasn't really that good." Or, "I'm so sorry you had to listen to me for that long. You didn't fall asleep when I was talking; that is IMPRESSIVE."

What was I really doing with comments like that? I was fishing for more compliments; that's what I was doing. When I receive a compliment and put myself down after hearing it, I'm really hoping the person will just compliment me again. Don't look at me like that. You do the same thing. No? Just me? I can live with that.

You know what I have started saying when someone compliments me about something? "Thank you for your kind words." When you try and deflect the compliments, you are taking the attention off the person encouraging and placing it squarely on yourself. I want the person encouraging me to feel good about what they said. I don't want them to feel like they have just entered into a counseling session they can never get out of. When someone encourages you, tell them thank you, sincerely. You don't need to deflect encouragement. It's ok to feel good about what you have done. In the church world especially, we have been taught to constantly deflect when someone says something nice to us, out of fear of "getting a big head."

I think this is harmful. I think it causes us to unnecessarily put ourselves down, and when we do that, all we are doing is fishing for more compliments anyway. If you are a Christ follower, can I ask you a question? Do you think God enjoys it when His children feel good about something they have done?

I love it when my kids feel good about themselves. When someone encourages one of my daughters, I don't expect them to say, "You know, thanks for the compliments about me getting good grades, but honestly, I was only able to get those good grades because my dad is so amazing." As true as that may be, I didn't earn those grades, she did.

I'm not saying we shouldn't live a life that is grateful. I'm saying it's ok to be proud of something you have done. I'm saying it's ok to say thank you when someone encourages you instead of deflecting. If you believe in God, don't you think He would want you to feel good about yourself? Don't you think He would want you to have a positive self-image?

If you are someone who longs to have your cup filled by others through encouragement, strive to be a person who speaks life into others on a consistent basis. Give away the very thing that you most long for. You know what you will soon discover? You will discover that speaking life into others in turn speaks life into you.

You will discover that not only are those words filling their tanks, your words will start to fill your own tank.

DIGGING FOR GOLD

I HAVE DISCOVERED THAT IT'S PRETTY EASY TO SPEAK KINDLY OF PEOPLE THAT YOU LIKE. Speaking encouragement toward people you don't is a bit more challenging. I want to challenge you to be a person who digs to find gold. What if you got paid $100 for every good thing you could think of that represents the person that you can't stand? They may drive you crazy. They may be lazy. You will never be their best friend. But they sure do know how to dress well. They are a good dad. They have a soul. They breathe air. They have a past. It's easy to notice the shortcomings of someone else. Everyone notices faults. You really want to be different? You really want to stand out and be unique? You can either get another tattoo, or you can be someone who is fanatical about encouraging others. I'm not anti tattoo, by the way. I'm just really, really pro speaking life. This is not normal. Our world doesn't live this way. Our culture doesn't live this way. Sadly, in large part, our churches don't operate this way either.

Nobody cares about your ego. Let's be people who are on a mission to build up what life has torn down. I want to make it my mission to pick up as many bricks each day as I possibly can and place them back on the wall they were knocked down from. I may not be able to rebuild the life of another person entirely on my own. It's not my job to rebuild the life of another person. It's my job to add a brick. Do you want to be a person who tears others down, or do you want to be someone who builds them back up? Chase better.

CHAPTER 10

COMMUNICATION

"You can have brilliant ideas, but if you can't get them across, your ideas won't get you anywhere."

—Lee Iacocca

EVERYONE'S LEAST FAVORITE DAY OF SCHOOL

WE ALL HAVE TWO THINGS IN COMMON. NONE OF US LIKE THE GUY WHO DRIVES SLOW IN THE fast lane, and all of us were terrified to give our first speech in front of a whole class during middle school. Do you remember speech class? I'm not sure if it was called speech, or English, or "How to pee yourself and be scarred for life 101." We all had that class. First of all, middle school was the absolute worst. You could not pay me enough money to go back to middle school. It is such an awkward time. All of the girls are taller than the boys. The boys smell because they are in the throws of their "I shower once every two weeks because I was bribed to" phase. Everyone is going through puberty. All the boys have little bodies and ginormous feet. Your voice cracks all the time, but especially when you are nervous. It's just an awkward time. Yet, somehow, we think that is a good time to have students stand in front of their peers to give a speech on the Revolutionary War.

Do you remember how you felt the night before your five-minute speech? Remember trying to invent new ways you could be sick in the morning? Is swine flu still a thing? Bird flu? Velociraptor flu?

Your time comes to give your speech, and you stand in front of your classmates that you are convinced are making fun of every single word you say. This could cripple you for life. One wrong pronunciation of one word could ruin your hallway cred for the next two years. This is life or death stuff. I joke, but it really did feel that way in junior high.

Most people are petrified of speaking in public. This isn't just something that junior high boys with B.O. and a Fortnight addiction deal with. Did you ever have that dream the night before a speech in middle school that you were standing in front of your class giving your speech and all of a sudden, you realize you are naked? Any time we think about talking in front of others, our minds almost immediately shift into the worst-case scenarios that we are convinced are going to become reality.

I don't have to spend a lot of time convincing you that most people are scared to talk in front of others. The truth is, this isn't just a fear most of us have in middle school and then grow out of as we get older. I'd venture to guess that the majority of adults are afraid to speak in public. And, even if they aren't full blown afraid of it, they definitely don't prefer it. If there was possibly a way to get out of speaking in public, most of us would find a way to get out of it. Swine flu? Bird Flu? Velociraptor flu? Let someone else do it?

THE DEATH OF SOMEONE ELSE

SOMEONE ELSE GETS VOLUNTEERED TO DO A LOT OF THINGS. WHEN I WAS A YOUNG PASTOR, we decided to do a mock funeral service during a Sunday morning. I used the passage from Exodus when God told Moses to stand before Pharaoh and tell him to "Let me people go." Moses had a problem. He stuttered and didn't like speaking in front of people, let alone the most powerful man in the world. He told God, "Let someone else do it." Someone else often gets volunteered to do the things that we don't want to do. In the service, I told the congregation that Mr. "Someone Else" wasn't with us anymore, so it was up to us to go talk with our friends about God or volunteer in the nursery.

Moses wasn't in junior high when he was embarrassed to stand in front of Pharaoh. He was actually about eighty years old. Being afraid to speak in public isn't usually something that people just grow out of. I fully understand that speaking in public is a very broad definition. Public can be whatever you define it as. Some people get nervous speaking in front of a crowd of two or three people. Others get nervous if it's more than 200. I always was fascinated by that. What is the magic number when you are no longer nervous to speak in front of others? If it's 199 people, I'm good. But, so help me, if it's 200 people.......

Why is it that most people get so nervous when speaking in front of others? The main reason is, we are self-conscious to a fault and want to be viewed in a positive light. This isn't a bad thing. I'm certainly not advocating being hated by others. I truly believe there are a few simple fixes to help all of us become better communicators. You may never be tasked with being a speaker on a stage in front of thousands of people. Few people are. Maybe being a better communicator for you means learning how to better get your point across to your boss about why you deserve a raise. Maybe for you, being a better communicator means learning how to talk to your spouse or your kids without losing your cool. Learning how to communicate well with others is vitally important.

THE ART OF COMMUNICATION

HUMANS AREN'T THE ONLY SPECIES THAT HAS LEARNED HOW TO COMMUNICATE WITH ITS own kind. Animals communicate with each other, too, but I think even the most hardcore animal people out there would admit that humans can communicate with each other better than animals can. We have thousands of different languages. We can communicate with words, body language, sign language, and Morse Code. We understand sarcasm and tone and humor. We can communicate with emotion and empathy. We can communicate with the written word or through pictures or song. We can even utilize technology to assist those with physical challenges who desire to communicate with others.

I don't think there is a person on Planet Earth who can, with any sort of confidence, say they have mastered everything there is to master about communication. Communication is a very broad term. All of us can chase better when it comes to communicating. Since most of us will probably never pursue a career in public speaking, let's talk about how to improve communication in your day-to-day life. I do believe anyone can get better at speaking in public. I don't believe a crowd of people has to terrify you. We aren't talking about being on a stage in a room full of people right now. We are talking about you, one on one with another person.

A lot of studies have been done about what percentage of our communication is verbal verses nonverbal. I don't want to get into exact percentages because I think it's impossible to define. I think we can all agree that not all communication is done with words. We communicate by listening. We communicate with body language. We communicate with signals, and we sometimes use words.

LEARNING HOW TO HELP OTHERS AWAKEN

WHEN WE TALK ABOUT BEING BETTER COMMUNICATORS, MOST OF US IMMEDIATELY THINK about how we can use words better. How can we enunciate better? How can we use emotion better? We very rarely think about how we can improve our body language. We DEFINITELY don't think very much about how we can improve our listening. If you are anything like me, I don't really listen very well. I just wait for you to stop talking so that I can start.

All of us care a lot about what we have to say. I'm not saying that's a bad thing. It's just reality. Your opinion is valuable. Your words are important. But your words and your opinion are not more important than the person or group that you are communicating with.

Do you want to know one thing that will help you greatly overcome your fear of communicating to groups of people? It's pretty simple, actually. Stop thinking about what people are going to think about you, and start thinking about the value you can bring to those who are listening. In others words, it's not about you; it's about them. Make it your mission to help people. If you are in communication with an individual, become fanatical about unlocking something hidden inside of them. I don't want that to sound dramatic. I honestly believe that there is greatness hidden inside everyone. Greatness is hidden inside my wife. Greatness is hidden inside my kids. Greatness is hidden inside you!

I've begun to ask myself a few important questions. The first question is, do I believe that greatness is hidden inside of each person? I can truthfully say the answer to that question is yes. The next question is, do I believe that I can assist that greatness to be unleashed in them? The answer to that is yes as well. So, I believe there is greatness inside of everyone. I believe that I can help pull that out of each person. The real question is how. How can you and I pull greatness out of everyone we meet?

Are people going to be changed because of listening to me talk? Maybe. Are people going to be awakened by hearing me share my opinion? Maybe. But doubtful. I truly believe that people don't need to be convinced of many things. They need to be awakened. If you are talked into something, you can be talked out of it. I don't want to use my communication skills to convince someone of anything. That's why I don't engage in Facebook debates. They are pointless. I don't want to change your mind. I don't want to convince you. My job isn't to awaken you to think like me. My job is to help you be awakened to the understanding that there truly is greatness inside of you. There is something inside of you that the world needs.

What awakens us? I think we are awakened when we start to believe. We are awakened when we stop fearing the worst. We are awakened when we believe change is possible. What does that have to do with you and me? What if you made it your mission every single day to communicate life to those you came in contact with. Your Starbucks barista. Your dry cleaner. Your lazy coworker. Your spouse and kids. What if life wasn't all about me? What if life was about serving whomever I am in relationship with? What if my mission was to awaken? I don't want to awaken you to think like me. I want to awaken others to believe in something. Life is much better when we are on mission. Your mission is probably different from mine. We all have a mission. What's yours? What makes you tick? That's what I want to help awaken in each person. Most people don't know what makes them tick. They don't know what makes them come alive. When we don't know what makes us come alive, it's easy to get bogged down with the day-to-day cares of a stressful and difficult life.

TELL LESS, UNDERSTAND MORE.

HOW MANY PEOPLE DO YOU COME IN CONTACT WITH EACH DAY WHO ARE OVERWHELMED

with life? How many people do you come in contact with every day that are an eleven on a scale of one to ten when it comes to stress? Open your eyes. There are people hurting all around you. Communicate with them. Don't add to their crappy day. Don't give them another reason to die a little on the inside.

You will communicate better when the focus of your communication changes from getting your point across to helping someone else awaken. How do we help someone awaken? By helping them take their focus off of whatever is happening in their life that is negative. We help awaken by being different. In a world that is filled with people who are desperate to share their opinion, dare to be someone who is different. We communicate much differently when the focus is less on getting our point across and more on understanding what the other person is trying to say.

If you are in sales, being a good communicator would be a good skill to have, agree? If you use your communication skills to talk someone into purchasing something that they don't really want, they won't be a customer very long. Good salespeople learn to be good communicators. They focus less on selling to the customer and more on learning what it is that the customer actually wants. Your mission as a salesperson isn't to sell a product. Your mission is to get someone what they want. If you help someone get what they want, they don't feel like they were sold anything. They are simply excited because they got what they wanted.

People don't want to be sold. They want to be understood. Almost all aspects of our economy are rooted in some sort of sales. This is what makes capitalism, capitalism. It's how our economy works. A value is placed on a product. That value is determined by what someone is willing to pay for it. That's why I don't focus a ton on price. I focus on value. What something costs truly doesn't matter. What matters is, how much does that thing bring value to my life? How bad do I want it? That's what matters more than what it costs.

VALUE MATTERS MORE THAN COST

IF YOU ARE IN ANY SORT OF BUSINESS, IT WOULD BE WISE FOR YOU TO LEARN THAT VERY basic principle. If I am trying to sell something, do you personally believe it's expensive? If you do, that will come across when you talk about it. Do you focus on cost, or do you focus on value? Think about your favorite experiences you have ever had when purchasing something. Did you feel like the person selling you whatever that was pressured you into buying it? Probably not. You felt understood. You felt prioritized. Let's not beat around the bush. You felt catered to. I don't care who you are, you desire to be catered to as well. You like the idea of flying first class. You want the fast passes at Disney. You like the way you feel when dining in a five-star restaurant instead of at a Cracker Barrel at 10:00 p.m. on a Tuesday night.

Liking those things doesn't make you a jerkface. It makes you pretty normal. This quote has been attributed to several different people, but I think it's most commonly attributed to Zig Ziglar. He said, "If you help enough people get what they want, you will have everything that you want."

He didn't say if you sell enough. He didn't say if you manipulate enough or talk enough people into purchasing something they don't want. He said if you help enough people get what THEY want, you'll have everything that you want.

Is your life centered around helping others get what they want? Do you wake up each day thinking about what kind of value you can bring to the world? Or are you just desperate to share how much you know?

Nobody likes that guy who is consistently talking about himself. Nobody grows up thinking they can't wait to be Facebook debate guy. I want to tell you this as nicely as I possibly can. The world doesn't care about you. They just don't. People don't want to spend hours looking at pictures of you. The only reason any of us want to look at pictures is to see if we are in them or not. It's just the truth. We are all good at faking being interested in something, and I'm not necessarily saying that is a bad thing. We all need to learn how to be polite even if we aren't feeling it on the inside.

People don't care about you. You know what people care about? People care about themselves.

WHAT NO ONE LIKES AND ALMOST EVERYONE DOES

CAN I BE REALLY HONEST? I'M REALLY BAD ABOUT INTERRUPTING PEOPLE WHEN THEY TALK. I alluded to this in a previous chapter. I am constantly finishing other people's sentences for them. I don't like that I do this, and it's honestly been something I have continuously been working on for the past year. First off, nobody likes that guy. I've had to ask myself some really hard questions. Why do I do that? Have you ever asked yourself that before? If you are someone like me who struggles with finishing someone else's sentences for them, why do you do that? I can't answer why you do that. I can tell you why I do. I do it because I want to feel important. I want to know things. I like the sound of my own voice. I do it without even thinking. Frankly, I do it because I'm not a very good listener.

I was the poster boy for listening so I could speak instead of being someone who listens so that I could understand. Do you want to know something that has really helped me to stop interrupting people and, quite frankly, stop talking so much? I ask questions. I ask a lot of questions. People in general really like talking about things they care about. And most people care about themselves. Small tip: If you want to learn how to be a better communicator, start talking about things you care about. You will always communicate best about the things that matter the most to you.

I have tried to become someone who focuses on asking people really good questions. I do this now for a couple of reasons. I want people to feel heard and understood when they are around me. I also want to better understand what makes them tick. How would I possibly know what makes someone tick if I am constantly looking for opportunities to talk? I honestly believe that every person can teach me something. I don't learn a whole lot when I am talking. I can learn a ton by listening, though. If you want to be better, if you want to be smarter, if you want to sell more, if you want to make more money, if you want to have a happier wife, and if you want your kids to adore you, don't be quick to share your opinion. Be quick to listen and eager to understand.

Obviously, part of communication is learning to use your words effectively. Words can be incredibly powerful. In the Bible, James says that life and death can be found in the tongue. I don't want to be overly dramatic about this, but you could make an argument that every word you speak is either speaking life or taking it away. I get it. We all participate in small talk. I'm not saying that chatting with your neighbor about yesterday's football game is speaking death to something. (Although I have been known to be a tad negative when it comes to the sports teams I follow.) I'm in the process of chasing better when it comes to my attitude toward my sports team. I'm a work in progress.

While I'm on the subject of sports, can I make a plea to you? Don't be that guy who sends hateful tweets to an athlete. Just don't be that guy. Don't be the guy who justifies doing so because that athlete makes millions and they should be able to take the criticism. Just don't be that guy. Is spouting off on Twitter about so and so striking out really adding value to your life? Is that honestly making you feel better? Just because a person has millions of dollars doesn't mean they now suddenly no longer have feelings. Of course you can be upset. Of course you can be frustrated. Those players have wives. They have children. Do you honestly want that star athlete's kids to see a tweet that you sent calling that player names? Do you want that athlete's mom reading that? Just stop. Full disclosure. I have vented on social media lamenting about my team before.

From the bottom of my heart Chicago Cubs, I apologize. I'm not perfect. Maybe that should be another theme of this book.

Technology has made communication easier and harder at the same time. It's easier because we have more opportunities to connect than we ever have. It's more difficult because we don't communicate face to face nearly as often as we used to. I'm all for technology. I use it every single day. I just know screens can't make another person come alive like interaction with another individual can.

GETTING OVER YOURSELF

DO YOU DESIRE TO COMMUNICATE BETTER? IF THE ANSWER TO THAT QUESTION IS YES, WHAT aspect of communication do you want to get better in? Do you want to be a better listener? Practice being a better listener. Observe how often you speak versus how often you listen. Force yourself to look into another person's eyes as they talk to you, instead of being distracted by a device. The first step to improving anything about yourself is awareness. We will never change anything about ourselves that we can't recognize. I have been interrupting people when they talk for the majority of my life. I didn't start making a change to stop until I realized I was doing that. Most people don't realize they are terrible listeners. They don't realize it because they are so wrapped up in their own little world. Is that you? Are you wrapped up in you? Is that something you want to change about yourself? Change it.

Do you find yourself getting nervous about speaking in front of a crowd of people whenever you get the opportunity? Is that something you would like to change? Those are important questions, because you won't ever change if it isn't something you desire. Do you have a stuttering issue? Go to a speech therapist. I don't care that you are forty-seven years old. Go get better! If someone can get braces at forty-three years old, you can see a speech therapist if that's what it takes. Can you not afford that? Go purchase some books that help you communicate better. There are literally THOUSANDS of books about communication. Can you not afford to buy books? Get a library card. The point is this: One thing that will never help you get better is making excuses. Stop focusing on what you can't do and start focusing on what you can. I almost typed start focusing on what you do do but I'm WAY too mature for that. Obviously.

Most people who are afraid to communicate don't have speech issues. They have "I care too much about what other people think" issues. If you ever get the opportunity to speak in front of others and you get insanely nervous, have you ever stopped to ask yourself why? Why are you nervous? I can almost guarantee you that the reason you are nervous is because you don't want to mess up, and you don't want to be perceived in a negative way.

As a former pastor, I'll admit that I used to be very critical of others when I heard them speak. I would instantly compare myself to them. Are they funnier than me? Are they more engaging? I would find myself retreating to my phone if I was ever in a service that I felt "didn't relate to me." Pretty selfish, right? I agree. Here's something I noticed about myself, anytime I heard someone talk who wasn't interesting to me, I would start looking at my phone. As soon as that person started sharing something vulnerable about themselves, I would lift my eyes from my phone and engage with the person on the stage. Why? We are drawn to people who are bold enough to be vulnerable.

If you desire to become a better communicator, I have two tips for you. The first is to communicate about something that you care about. The second is to be willing to be vulnerable. You don't have to bare your soul. You don't have to share your deepest, darkest secret. Your goal when communicating is to connect to the heart of another person. It doesn't matter if you are speaking to five people or five thousand people. You are attempting to communicate to the heart of another person. There is nothing that communicates to the heart of another person like a person sharing something vulnerable about themselves. Why? Because we all know what it is like to struggle. We all know what it is like to feel like we don't measure up. If you want to chase better at communicating, communicate vulnerably about things that you care about. Think less about what people are going to think about you and more about the heart of the person who needs to hear the message that is lying dormant inside of you. You have a message inside of you that the world needs to hear. Get over yourself. Get past your insecurity. Be willing to be vulnerable. Nobody wants you to be a perfect speaker who pronounces every word correctly. They want you to be your gloriously imperfect self.

CHAPTER 11

THE BEST PARKING ATTENDANT IN THE WORLD

"Your life does not get better by chance. It gets better by change."

—Jim Rohn

HAPPY PLACE

I LOVE BASEBALL MORE THAN JUST ABOUT ANYTHING. WRIGLEY FIELD IN CHICAGO IS MY happy place. When I lived in Southwest Florida, March was one of my favorite times of the year. There are no hurricanes. It isn't 4578 degrees out. You don't sweat going to check the mail, and baseball is starting. The Boston Red Sox and Minnesota Twins spring train each year in the Fort Myers area, which is where I lived for the vast majority of my 20's and 30's. I would get the chance to go to two or three games each season. There is nothing like going to a baseball game. The smells. The sound of a baseball cracking off a bat or being caught by a leather glove. It's truly the closest thing to heaven on earth.

A few years ago, I was heading with a friend to a Red Sox spring training game on a beautiful March afternoon. Traffic in Southwest Florida is always pretty rough, but it's especially rough during "snowbird" season, which is what local residents affectionately call seasonal residents who clog up the roads. Local residents tend to love that tourists and seasonal residents come and spend their money. They aren't big fans of them coming and driving on their roads, however. March just so happens to be smack dab in the middle of snowbird season. And spring break season. And baseball spring training season. Needless to say, traffic in Southwest Florida in March is heavy. I've never in my life met anyone who enjoys traffic delays. The worst parts of us tend to come out during traffic delays.

Not only do we not enjoy traffic delays, I've never met a single person who loves paying for parking. Any time you go to a professional sporting event, you not only have to pay a ton for a ticket to watch the game live, but you also have to pay to park your vehicle. I get it. Most people aren't in the best of moods when they have waited twenty or thirty minutes in stand still traffic, only to get to the parking lot and have to pay $20 to watch people practice playing baseball. I'm not bitter, I promise. This is just an observation.

Being a parking lot attendant has to be an interesting job. Almost all of the attendants in Southwest Florida are retired guys from the Northeast with stereotypical Boston accents. They sit out there all day dealing with people's attitudes in the searing heat for minimum wage at best. I'm sure, for them, it's a chance to stay busy, get out of the house, and be close to the game of baseball for thirty days during spring training. I'll be honest, I don't notice most parking lot attendants. People don't pay money to watch parking lot attendants. They are necessary. But they certainly aren't the attraction.

On this particular March day, traffic was unusually bad. I sat in line, paid my money to park my car, and proceeded to pull into the parking lot at Jet Blue Park in Fort Myers, which is the spring training home of the

Boston Red Sox. As I pulled my car into the grass field, I saw a parking attendant about 150 yards away. There was a car in front of me that the attendant was guiding into his spot. I had my window down after just paying to park so I could hear the attendant. After he parked the car in front of me, my car was now about 100 yards away. I heard him start talking to me. He obviously didn't know my name, so he called me be the name and color of my vehicle.

"Gray Kia. I got you, man. Seventy-five more yards. That is beautiful. You are a great driver. Keep coming. Almost there, man. Turn your wheel a little to the left. Fifty more yards. Man, this is great. Almost there. Little bit more. BAM. Right there. Nicely done, my friend. Enjoy the game."

As soon as my car was parked, he began to do the same thing to the cars behind me. There was a crowd of people gathered to watch this guy park cars in a parking lot. They were skipping their chance to watch professional baseball players take batting practice so that they could watch a guy in his late 60's park cars in a grass parking lot.

I told the guy who was with me that I would pay that guy to be in charge of parking at our church. I learned something that day from this random, retired parking attendant. No matter what you do, you can always give your best and show enthusiasm. Enthusiasm is contagious. It doesn't really matter what you are doing. You can be doing the most mundane thing you can imagine. If you do that mundane task with enthusiasm, people will notice. I have no doubt that parking attendant put a smile on hundreds of people's faces that day. This happened three years ago, and I'm still talking about it.

LOVING WHAT YOU DO

SEVENTY-FIVE PERCENT OF AMERICANS DON'T LIKE THEIR JOBS. THINK ABOUT THAT FOR A second. Three out of four people are miserable at their place of employment. Most people change jobs thinking that will help them to be happier, only to discover that stress tends to follow us wherever we go. Certainly, some jobs are more stressful than others. I just tend to believe that if your life has purpose, what you do doesn't define you nearly as much as who you are.

I don't think the man parking cars felt he was operating in his life calling. I don't think he went to car parking school. I think he is a man who is determined to give his best at no matter what he does. I'm guessing he is happy. I'm guessing his grandkids adore him. I'm guessing he's just happy to be around the game of baseball for a few days. I want to be like that guy.

How about you? Are you happy right now? Be honest. Do you look more forward to Friday than you do to Monday? Why is that? Is it because we just really look forward to the weekend, or is it that we really dread being at a job we can't stand for five more days? Most people endure work for fifty weeks out of the year and center their whole year around two weeks of vacation time. Vacation is great. We all should have things on the calendar each year that we look forward to. We just shouldn't have to dread all the other days.

FRED THE POSTMAN

ONE OF THE BOOKS THAT HAS HAD A HUGE IMPACT ON MY LIFE IS ONE BY MARK SANBORN called *Fred Factor*. In the book, the author talks about his postman named Fred. As a professional speaker who is often on the road, Mark would be gone for days at a time. Fred the postman knew that and would go out of his way to make sure that he held onto Mark's mail for him until he returned. Fred never left packages on the doorstep but instead put them under mats or behind the house so that nobody from the street would see packages on the doorstep insinuating someone wasn't home. There are two words that we use to describe people like Fred the postman and the best parking attendant in the world. "Above" and "beyond." The parking attendant wouldn't have lost his job if he hadn't put in the amount of enthusiasm that he did. Fred would have been a perfectly normal postman if he did what he was paid to do—put the mail in the mail box and leave the packages on the front door with a little sticker on the front door. They both went above and beyond.

I bet neither felt as if they were operating in their professional life calling. Fred probably didn't grow up thinking about becoming a postman. The parking attendant didn't dream of being a parking attendant. They both just chose to go above and beyond and let who they were shine above what they did.

You know what I have learned about people who go above and beyond what is asked of them? They are almost always happy people. They aren't any different from you and me. They have bills. They have people who push their buttons. They don't like waiting in line at the DMV. They just have something inside of them that doesn't allow them to do things halfway. Doing enough to just get by doesn't compute to them.

People who do things halfway on a consistent basis are rarely happy people. People who do things halfway are never happy. They seem to always be biding their time waiting for something else. They punch a clock at work waiting for 5 o'clock to come around. Most people who are halfway people aren't happy, and it's not because of what they do for work. Halfway people generally don't like who they are. They may mask that with insecurity or humor or some other sort of vice. When you don't like who you are, you rarely ever go above and beyond for anything. Life just seems like a sentence to be paid as opposed to a gift to be enjoyed.

DEPRESSION

I WANT TO SHARE A QUOTE WITH YOU. IT'S CONTROVERSIAL. BEFORE I POST THIS QUOTE, please let me say that I don't always agree with this quote. It's not my quote. I fully understand that there are people and situations this doesn't apply to. Depression is a real thing. Depression can be a clinical thing. More people take their lives because of depression now than at any time in history. Monthly, it seems as if another celebrity has reportedly taken their own life. We hear reports of military personnel coming home from their missions and of many taking their own lives. I don't believe that everyone who is depressed is depressed by choice. I totally get that. When I share this quote, please know that I am fully aware this may not apply to you.

I do believe there are some people that deal with depression not because its clinical, but because it is a choice. Are you ready for the quote? Here it is.

"The seeds of depression can never take root in a grateful heart."

—Andy Andrews

I understand this may not apply to you. What if it does, though? How do you feel about life? Is it a gift? Or is it just something you are trying to make it through? I don't know what it is like to be you. I don't know about your past. I don't know about your stress. I don't know about your family. I do know that if you are alive, you have been given a tremendous gift. You have been given the gift of being alive. None of us got to choose the hand that we were dealt when we were born. We didn't choose our parents. We didn't choose our nationality. We didn't choose our race or our gender.

You may not agree with the above quote, but I think there is one thing we can agree on: People who approach life as a gift are much happier than those who approach life as a grind. Do you want to know the honest truth? Life is a grind sometimes. I have good days and bad days. I have moments when I find myself being depressed. Do you want to know what helps me? I begin to think about all of the things that I have to be thankful for.

BLACK FRIDAY SHENANIGANS

AREN'T WE AS AMERICANS FUNNY PEOPLE? YOU COULD MAKE AN ARGUMENT THAT Thanksgiving is the happiest day on the entire calendar. There aren't presents exchanged. It's just a day centered around food, football, and thankfulness. Most people are pretty happy on Thanksgiving Day. We get to be around family. We laugh. We remember. We share reasons we have to be thankful. And when the day is done, Black Friday is here, and we instantly switch from being thankful to furious because someone cut in front of us in line at Walmart to buy the last fifty-inch plasma TV. People get trampled on Black Friday every single year. It's truly so sad. How can we go from being grateful one minute to lacking completeness the next because of a $400 TV? You know what's ironic? Most people who go Black Friday shopping aren't shopping for gifts for other people. They are there purchasing things for themselves.

Of course it isn't wrong to purchase something for yourself. It's just wrong to trample someone else to get it three hours after you just spent time being thankful for everything that you have been given. When was the last time you honestly spent time thinking of all the reasons you have to be thankful? Have you ever written them out? What if somebody paid you $10,000 if you could come up with a list of 100 things that you were genuinely grateful for? What if someone paid you $10,000 if you could write down 100 things that you genuinely liked about yourself? Do you think you could do it? Of course you could. I can't think of anything more important for you to do today than to take some time and physically start writing down lists. What is it in your life that is causing the most stress right now? Money? Your family? Your job? The things that aren't going well are well documented. I want to know what is going well.

Something happens inside of us when we take our attention off of what isn't going well and place it on something that is. Have you ever noticed that most people almost instantly go negative when you ask them a simple question like, "Hey, how are you?"

If you ask someone how the diet is going, "It's going well, but I cheated last weekend."
If you ask someone how the job is going, "It's going ok, but my boss is driving me crazy."
If you ask someone how the church is going, "It's ok, but giving has been down the last month."

Why do we do that? Monitor yourself this week. I want you to see how long it takes before your mind instantly starts to drift negative. Ask people questions this week, and watch how long it takes for them to start being negative. What if chasing better was as simple as forcing ourselves to see the good in almost every situation. I say almost because there are horrible things that happen in this world. There are always exceptions. Even in the worst situations that happen, I cannot change things that happen to me, but I can always change how I respond to those situations.

SUBTITLES

TO BE HONEST, WRITING THIS BOOK WASN'T AS CHALLENGING AS I THOUGHT IT WOULD BE. As it turns out, the mind is a pretty strong thing. We can do amazing things if we just commit to doing the work regardless of how we feel. One of the most difficult parts of the book that I admittedly overthought was the subtitle. The title was easy. The subtitle was a challenge. I legitimately wrestled back and forth with about fifty different options. Every person whom I asked seemed to like a different option. I didn't like any of them. Apparently in a book, the subtitle is just as important as the title itself. The subtitle has to somehow be a one-sentence summary of what the book is about. It has to grab your attention and make you want to choose that specific book in a sea of thousands of other books in the exact same genre.

One morning, I woke up, and the elusive subtitle that I was searching for appeared in my head for the first time. I knew that was what I wanted the heart of this book to truly be about. I'll save you the hassle of going back to the front cover of this book to see the subtitle.

"Awakening the person you've always longed to be."

That person is inside of all of us. Have you ever thought about the person you want to become? Aren't they amazing? Future me is so awesome. You should meet him someday.

What does the person you want to be look like, and how far away from that person are you right now? Do you honestly think that one day you are just going to wake up and be that person? Is becoming that person important to you? If becoming that person isn't important to you, you'll never meet them. More importantly, the world will never meet them.

I am on a relentless pursuit to awaken the me that I've always longed to be. The first step toward awakening that person was to define that person. If you don't know what you are chasing, you shouldn't be surprised when you never catch them. Maybe you aren't the person you want to be because you don't know the person you want to be.

Maybe it's time for you to figure that out. You may be miles away from the person you want to be. At least you have that person defined. You can't chase something you can't see or define.

What kind of income does future you earn? What is your demeanor like? How does future you treat people? What do future you's kids say about you? What does future you's spouse say about you?

I've already talked about him in this book, but one of my inspirations is Ed Mylett. Ed talks a lot about this subject in his podcasts. One of the things that he said, which has become my lifelong mission, is that at the end of his life, he wants the person he is striving to be and the person he actually is to be the same person.

I have to believe that is possible. What happens if the person you long to be never gets uncovered? How many people's lives could be impacted by future you that currently aren't being impacted by right-now you? I'm sure you are impacting some people now. Is that good enough for you? I am on a fanatical quest to awaken the me I have always longed to be.

I want to get closer and closer to that person every day, and each day is a practice field filled with opportunities. I have opportunities to get closer to that person when I am stuck in traffic. I have opportunities to get closer to that person when I see someone in line at the grocery store putting food back at the checkout line because they don't have the money to get everything they desire. Maybe you have enough money right now to afford the lifestyle that you want. What about the sea of humanity that is outside your doors right now struggling to survive? What if the more money you had meant the more people you could help?

What if I wasn't short with my kids today? What if I sat down and listened intently to how my wife's day was today instead of being distracted by everything else? What if, today, when someone asks me how things are going, I absolutely refused to allow myself to go in the direction of negative?

CHASING BETTER EVERY DAY

CHASING BETTER ISN'T DIFFICULT. CHASING BETTER EVERY DAY IS DIFFICULT. MOST OF US can do anything for a few days. Anyone can diet for a few days. Anyone can go to the gym for a few days. Anyone can be positive for a few days. What if you made yourself a negativity jar? What if, for the next thirty days, every time you say something negative, you have to put $5 in the jar. It needs to be an amount that you feel. This isn't the quarter cuss jar. After those thirty days are up, take all of the money in the jar and give it as a donation to the political party that you oppose. How's that for an out-of-the-box idea? I dare you. Yes, I know. Whichever political side you fall on, the other side is the enemy. I wish it wasn't that way. That's just the world we live in. Maybe you can't fathom giving a dime to that party. Good. This challenge should be easy for you, then. Spend thirty days saying nothing negative at all and see how you feel about yourself at the end.

Anyone can give money to a cause they care about. Maybe chasing better means thinking differently about the people with whom you most strongly disagree. There will always be people I disagree with. There will always be people I don't like. I don't treat those people with respect because they deserve it. They may not. I treat them with respect because I don't like what treating them with disrespect does to me.

CHAPTER 12

SHUT UP
AND DANCE

"The biggest hurdle in life is getting over yourself. Once you get over yourself, you can get anywhere."

—Tony Gaskins

DORKY WHITE GUY

IF YOU LOOK UP "PASTY WHITE DUDE WITH NO RHYTHM" IN THE DICTIONARY, YOU'LL SEE A picture of me with two thumbs up, smiling awkwardly at the camera. I've never been accused of being a great dancer. My first experience with dancing was back in junior high. We had school dances, and I was never really big with the ladies in junior high. Junior high is such an awkward time for everyone. If you go to a dance at most middle schools or high schools, you will see two groups of people. There is a group hanging around the perimeter of the dance floor, and you will see the other group on the dance floor.

If you are an adult and go to a party today where there is dancing, you will see those same groups of people. A dance floor is kind of like a television set in a living room. Everything in the room is pointed at the TV, and, at a dance, everything is pointed at the dance floor. If you are at a place where there is dancing, you are either standing around the perimeter of the dance floor, or you are out there dancing yourself with your friends.

For thirty-five years of my life, I took up residence on the perimeter. I can't speak for all of those who are perimeter people, and I realize I will be speaking mainly in generalizations. Some people aren't dancing simply because they don't like to dance. That's what I told myself. I was like a little kid who thought a game was stupid. Only, I didn't think the game was stupid at all; I loved the game. I just didn't like that I lost.

I didn't think dancing was stupid. I thought I was stupid. I thought I was uncoordinated. I was convinced that if I went out onto the dance floor everybody would stare at me. Somebody would film it on YouTube, and it would get ten million hits with the title of "What Was This Guy Thinking?"

The two most popular reasons people don't dance at events are:

- They don't think they know how to dance.
- They are afraid of what people will think.

Do we honestly believe that people think about us constantly? Subconsciously, I think we do. What if the dance floor was the key to you unlocking freedom in your life? It helped unlock mine.

When I started putting together the blueprint for this book, I listed out all of the chapters and what I wanted to write about. These were all areas I was incredibly passionate about. I wanted to end the book by talking about an area of my life that I felt I was terrible in that I was able to improve. In March of 2018, this pasty white guy with no rhythm enrolled in dance classes. I asked my wife Julie what she thought, and, just like with almost every other crazy and spontaneous idea I have, she was on board with it. She even agreed to go to some of the classes with me.

I picked up the phone and called the Arthur Murray Dance Studio in Lexington, Kentucky, where I live. A nice lady picked up the phone, and I just laid it all out there.

"I'm a dorky white guy with no rhythm. I'm writing a book about how to get better at things in life, and I want to be a good dancer. I don't just want to be adequate. I want to stand out. I'm going to be a project, but I can promise nobody in that dance studio will work harder than me."

There was silence on the other end of the phone, followed by laughter. The girl on the other end proceeded to tell me she had never had anyone want to sign up for dance classes for that reason. She asked me for my name, and I told her Corey, but that she could call me Dorky White Guy. I actually asked her to write Dorky White Guy down for my first lesson, which she did.

I showed up for my first lesson and was introduced to my instructor, Rosie. I could tell when I walked in, she was wondering who the heck this guy was who insisted on being called Dorky White Guy. She listened to what I wanted. I wanted to go from zero rhythm at all to being someone who stood out on a dance floor.

As we began to go through basic moves, I think she began to understand that she had her work cut out with me. She began to teach me basic moves for Salsa, Meringue, Jitter Bug, Hustle, Mamba and a few others I can't even remember. I told you, I had a lot to learn. We started practicing for a routine that was going to be taking place at the dance studio in a few weeks. As the lessons continued, I started to get more comfortable. I certainly didn't feel great with my style, but I was confident that I knew the moves and at the very least wasn't going to make a fool out of myself.

We did the routine on a Saturday morning. The song I chose was "Dynamite" by Taio Cruz. We only danced for a little over a minute. There were maybe 100 people there watching, and, much to my surprise, I wasn't nervous at all. There were actual judges there, people who have been dancing for a long time. We did the routine, people clapped, and it was over. Nobody filmed it and put it on Youtube to make fun of me—at least, not that I know of. Everyone was very supportive. I even had a number pinned to my back so that the judges could easily identify me so they could tell me the areas in which I could improve.

The next week, Rosie went over my scores with me, and, much to my surprise, they weren't horrible. She actually spent a lot more time telling me the things I did well then she did telling me the things I didn't. And there were plenty of those. Shouldn't that tell us something? We spend too much time trying to tell our kids or tell our students or tell our employees or spouses what they are doing wrong. What if the real motivation for them was you spending time telling them what they are doing right? Whatever gets rewarded gets repeated.

Rosie telling me that I had actually done a few things really well encouraged me to keep going back. Guilt and shame don't motivate anyone to want to change, at least not for the long haul. Rosie even told me how surprised she was that I had picked up on things so fast. She found the things I was doing well and encouraged me. I don't know if she meant it or not. I think she did. She may say the same thing to all her students. I just know she's a great teacher for two reasons. First, because she finds what her students are doing well and encourages them. Second, because she puts up with me.

Why is Rosie able to be so patient trying to teach a pasty white guy like me with no rhythm how to dance? It's actually pretty simple. It's because she loves to dance, and she's really good at it. When you love something that you have a talent for, you want to share that with others.

WHAT CAN YOU DO?

ALL OF US HAVE STRENGTHS AND WEAKNESSES. WE ALL HAVE AREAS IN WHICH WE CAN GET better. We can all get better in every area. The question really is, do we desire to chase better? What is an area of your life that you are intimidated to change? What if you committed to getting better at your greatest area of shortcoming? It may not be something fun like dancing. Maybe you have a really bad habit you are trying to overcome. Maybe it's one of the things I talked about in an earlier chapter. Maybe you are just really bad with money or your health journey is not the best. Maybe you care way too much about what others think about you, or the relationships that are the most important to you are shaky.

Maybe you can't afford to hire a coach like Rosie to help you get better at whatever it is you want to improve. Don't let that be an excuse to stay the same. Napoleon Dynamite didn't have money either. He rented a VHS tape that taught him how to dance, and that ended up getting Pedro elected president of the entire school.

I'm sure you can list a million reasons why you can't do something. You can list a million reasons why you can't change. Why you can't grow. Why you can't improve. It takes much mental strength to be negative. What if you stopped using all of the energy it takes to talk yourself into not doing something and started asking, "How can I do this?" What if the limitations you have weren't limitations but instead opportunities to be creative?

Change is never easy. That's why most people dislike change. We like to stick to the status quo. It's easier. It's less painful. It's way less personal. It's so much easier to blame. I don't want to live that way anymore. I'm committed to chasing better. I'm committed to finding the best version of me.

If life was a dance floor, where would you be standing? Are you someone standing around the perimeter with a drink in your hand, watching and judging everyone else on the dance floor? Or are you dancing? I love the lyrics to the Song "Shut up and Dance" by Walk the Moon.

"Oh don't you dare look back Just keep your eyes on me I said you're holding back She said shut up and dance with me."

I can actually picture the guy this song is talking about. I was that guy. I spent way too many years of my life looking backward. I spent way too many years of my life not seeing. The girl in this song is encouraging the guy to get out of his own head. To stop the excuses. To shut up and dance with me.

SHUT UP!

WHAT IF LIFE WAS MAKING THE SAME PLEA TO YOU AND I TODAY? JUST STOP. I KNOW WE aren't supposed to say shut up. But shut up. And start dancing. Shut up, stop the excuses, stop the negativity, stop the reasons why you can't. Shut up and dance with me. When life is all said and done, do you want to be the person watching with a drink, or do you want to be the person dancing? I've never in my life seen someone on a dance floor who wasn't having a good time. I've seen tons on the perimeter who weren't having a whole lot of fun. I've seen a ton of people standing on the perimeter looking at their watches, wondering when the next thing on the schedule would come up so they could go do something else. Refusing to live in the moment. Dance floors are kind of like casinos. Time doesn't matter. You don't see clocks in a casino, and you hardly ever see people on the dance floor checking their watches. When you are on the dance floor, you aren't thinking about what is next. You are thinking about enjoying the moment you have with those who matter the most to you.

Every person has two driving forces. We have our why that pushes us forward and our concepts that hold us back. Our why is what encourages us to get onto the dance floor. Our concepts keep us on the sidelines.

Picture yourself standing in a massive field. In the middle of the field, there is a massive wall as far as the eye can see. It is clear that the only way you will get to the other side of that wall is by scaling it. There is no getting around it. Why would you want to even get to the other side in the first place? The side of the wall you are on represents where you are now. You are comfortable. You are content. You are surviving.

The other side of the wall represents the person you want to be. It represents the life you want to live. The house you want to live in. The car you want to drive. The job you want to have. The income you want to earn.

There is a big obstacle that is standing in your way in the form of a giant wall. You really have two choices. Some people look at that wall and think to themselves, "I'm going to do whatever it takes to get over that wall." Others look at the obstacle and think, "There is no way in the world I am going to get over that wall."

Why can two different people look at the exact same obstacle and see two completely different things? It's actually pretty simple. One person focuses on the wall. One person focuses on what is on the other side of that wall. Whatever you consistently focus on will eventually become your reality. If you focus on the why, you will figure out how. If you consistently focus on the obstacle, you will consistently make excuses.

CAUTION TO THE WIND

WHEN IT COMES TIME FOR YOU TO JUMP INTO A POOL OF WATER, WHICH TYPE OF PERSON are you? Are you a toe dipper, or are you someone who throws caution to the wind, peels off the bandaid, and does a cannonball, Porter style, like the character from *The Sandlot*?

How many of us approach our life like we are tiptoeing into a pool that is chilly? When you are entering into a pool that you think is cold, entering the water slowly actually makes it colder. Just jump in, baby. That's the only way to go.

What area of your life are you standing around the perimeter in? Why are you standing there? Don't give the answer that makes you sound better than you really are. What is the real answer? Are you standing on the sidelines because you enjoy standing on the sidelines? Or are you standing there because you are afraid? If you enjoy standing on the sidelines, that's all well and good, but I don't think someone who enjoys standing on the sidelines would pick up a book called *Chasing Better*.

I hope that you decide to relentlessly pursue your best self. I don't know what that looks like for you. I have learned that there is much freedom that comes from taking personal responsibility for your current situation. If you are standing on the sidelines in a current area of your life, you are standing there by choice.

When you come to the end of your life, what will people remember you by? What will your legacy be? Do you want people to remember you for your passivity or for passion? Do you want people to remember how well you held a drink standing on the perimeter, or do you want people to remember your willingness to dance?

You aren't the best in the world. There will always be someone who looks better, makes more, drives a faster car, has more money in their 401k, and can afford nicer vacations than you. I'm not the most talented guy. This probably isn't the best book that you've ever read. I'm not the best speaker in North America. I'm just better than I was yesterday. And that's okay with me.

My hope for you is that finding your best self would start to become your number one goal in life. Your obsession will eventually become your reality. The problem is, we obsess over the wrong things. We obsess over the obstacles instead of obsessing over what is on the other side of overcoming those obstacles. I hate to break it to you—this isn't easy. If you strive to become your best self, there will be setbacks. There will be disappointments. If you are anything like me, you hold yourself to a very high standard and aren't very good at giving yourself very much grace.

You are capable of way more than you give yourself credit for. Do you want to train for an ironman competition? What's stopping you? Do you want to be a millionaire? What's stopping you? What is it that you want? What excuses have you been allowing yourself to believe that have kept you on the sidelines instead of taking a few steps toward the dance floor?

We all need people in our lives who tell us the truth. I don't know you. I don't know your past. I don't know all of the cards that have been stacked against you. I'm certain life most likely hasn't been fair to you. People have hurt you. People have wronged you. People have disappointed you. What are you going to do with that? We all teach our kids manners. Most of us probably teach our kids it isn't polite to say shut up. Maybe I should have put a PG-13 warning on the cover of this book. I'm going to say this anyway: If you want to succeed in life, if you want to chase better, shut up and start dancing. Stop the excuses. Stop thinking about all the reasons you can't. Stop thinking about everything that is stacked against you. Don't you dare keep looking back. Keep your eyes fixed on the goal that you have and the person you are striving to be. It's time to dance.

APPENDIX

A QUICK THOUGHT ABOUT BOOK AND PODCAST SUGGESTIONS: I MAKE IT A HABIT TO READ and listen to things that challenge the way I think. Don't make the mistake of dismissing something because you may disagree with some of the principles you read or listen to. Let's learn how to chew on meat, spit out bones, and allow ourselves to be willing to learn from people who have amazing things to teach us if we would just be willing to listen.

BOOK SUGGESTIONS

- *Do the Work* – Steven Pressfield
- *Girl, Wash Your Face* – Rachel Hollis
- *Willpower Doesn't Work* – Benjamin Hardy
- *Fred Factor* – Mark Sanborn
- *Rich Dad Poor Dad* – Robert Kiyosaki
- *Start* – Jon Acuff
- *Finish* – Jon Acuff
- *Be Obsessed or Be Average* – Grant Cardone
- *10X Rule* – Grant Cardone
- *Necessary Endings* – Dr. Henry Cloud
- *Relentless* – Tim Grover
- *Love Does* – Bob Goff
- *Start with Why* – Simon Sink
- *Deep Work* – Cal Newport
- *You are a Badass* – Jen Sincero (Yes, I'm aware this is a "swear word." Read this book anyway.)
- *Eat That Frog* – Brian Tracy

- *Ordering Your Private World* – Gordon MacDonald
- *Teammate* – David Ross
- *The Power of Focus* – Jack Canfield, Mark Victor Hansen, Les Hewitt
- *The One Thing* – Gary Keller
- Total Money Makeover – Dave Ramsey
- 5 Love Languages – Gary Chapman

PODCAST SUGGESTIONS

- Ed Mylett Show
- Cardone Zone
- The GaryVee Audio Experience
- The Andy Stanley Leadership Podcast
- School of Greatness with Lewis Howes
- The Robcast
- The BiggerPockets
- The Joe Rogan Experience
- The Tony Robins Podcast

ACKNOWLEDGEMENTS

I WILL NEVER FORGET SITTING IN A CONFERENCE IN LAS VEGAS AND LISTENING TO A BUNCH of communicators share their ideas with huge crowds of people. I remember listening to each of them and thinking, not so humbly, to myself, "I could do so much better than these guys."

Is that arrogant? Probably. It's just true. Almost instantly after thinking that thought, I had another thought: "Maybe you could do it better. Maybe you couldn't. But they are doing it, and you are not."

I have wanted to write a book for as long as I can remember. I can't tell you how many times I have shared with people that I am writing a book, and they have responded with some sort of, "I have always wanted to do that."

I came home from that conference and decided to write, and, twelve weeks later, the manuscript for *Chasing Better* was complete.

I am grateful for those people in my life who inspire me to Chase Better every single day. Some of them know who I am. Some of them have no idea who I am.

- Thank you to my amazing wife, Julie, who puts up with me on a daily basis. This is no small task. Thanks for your patience with my crazy ideas and for loving me in spite of my many faults.
- Thank you to Addison and Sadie. You are my world, and being your dad is one of my greatest joys.

- Thank you to my family. To my parents for teaching me how to love and how to work. To my brothers for always being there to bring me back down to earth. Hanging out with you truly is one of my greatest joys.
- Thank you to Amy Thomas for your amazing editorial skills and for making me sound better than I really am.
- Thank you to Jeremy Wells for your amazing skill in graphic design and video creation.
- Thank you to my amazing friends and business partners, Dan Valentine, Doug Wood, Eric Hunsberger, Terri Miller, and many, many more. You have all changed my life in so many ways, and I will be forever grateful.
- To my many close, personal friends, thank you. You know who you are, and your support means everything.
- Thank you to the Chicago Cubs. I admit, I am a pessimistic sports fan. Thank you for daily entertainment. Thank you for Wrigley Field. Thank you for a World Series win. Thank you for teaching me about loyalty.

Last but not least, I'm grateful for you. Thanks for taking the time to read this book. I know there are literally millions of books out there. Thanks for choosing this one. If this book inspired you in any way, recommend it to a friend. I would be forever grateful. ☺